Get Covered!

How to craft, pitch and tell your startup's story to get more customers.

RENÉE WARREN &
CRYSTAL RICHARD

Renée Warren & Crystal Richard
Copyright © 2018 Crystal Richard & Company Inc.

All rights reserved.
No part of this book may be reproduced, stored in a retrieval system, or transmitted in any form or by any means (photocopying, electronic, mechanical, recording and other), without the prior written permission of the authors.

ISBN-13: 978-1981911738
ISBN-10: 1981911731

www.getcoveredbook.com

DEDICATIONS

To my husband, for believing in me since the day we met on Twitter, and to my family for supporting me in all my endeavours.
Renée Warren

To mom and dad for buying me my first typewriter. To Dan for the toffee nut lattes and love that make this book and so much more possible.
Crystal Richard

CONTENTS

Foreword		i
Chapter 1:	Understanding Public Relations	3
Chapter 2:	Executing a Winning PR Strategy: Two Case Studies	10
Chapter 3:	Are You Ready for PR?	22
Chapter 4:	Crafting the Ultimate Story	35
Chapter 5:	The Press Release - Why It Still Exists, and How to Use It	47
Chapter 6:	Establishing Goals and Tracking Your PR Efforts	56
Chapter 7:	Start Building Rapport Early	69
Chapter 8:	Perfecting The Pitch	80
Chapter 9:	Be Prepared: Are You Ready for When the Media Comes Knocking?	99
Chapter 10:	Gaining Traction When the Media Won't Cover You	114
Chapter 11:	You've Secured Coverage, Now What?	120
Chapter 12:	The Continuing Role of PR	127
	Conclusion	131
	Acknowledgments	134
	Appendix	138

Get Covered!

FOREWORD

> *"If I was down to my last dollar, I would spend it on Public Relations."*
> \- BILL GATES

No matter what your industry or which stage of growth you're in- one thing is certain: you need your company to be noticed.

After all, publicity is vital for your survival and for ensuring your success.

But if you're anything like most startups, there's a good chance you're a bit confused and possibly overwhelmed by the concept of public relations. It's understandable; after all, it's an industry that's filled with jargon and conflicting advice. Flip open any book on PR, and you'll find any number of tactics that different professionals swear by.

Who's right? Which way is best? And what does it all mean anyway?

If you're looking for some quick tricks to hack your way into the news, then this isn't the book for you. But if you're hoping for a guide that will take you through the proven strategies that PR professionals, as well as startups and everyday business owners alike are using to build solid PR strategies; ones that generate results, then keep reading.

In our years of helping startups to make their big breaks, we've discovered a lot about PR. We learned that it's not always the flashiest campaign or even the most exciting news that wins in the game of press coverage, at the end of the day it's about your story; and how well you're able to tell it.

Although PR has changed considerably throughout the years and will continue to do so into the future, some tenets of it will always remain the same. It's these timeless principles that we've expounded upon in this book. We've also shared some tips for real-world execution. For telling that your story and getting noticed. For standing out in today's digital age.

It's our goal to show you exactly what it will take to get your company covered. We hope that this book will serve as your field guide for navigating the often-confusing world of PR.

CHAPTER 1

UNDERSTANDING PUBLIC RELATIONS

"PR is a mix of journalism, psychology, and lawyering - it's an ever changing and always interesting landscape."
- RONN TOROSSIAN, FOUNDER SW PUBLIC RELATIONS

As a startup, you don't need us to tell you that you're different from the big guys.

From having a smaller operating budget and the need to make decisions that will result in immediate revenue, to the frantic struggle to shine some light on a largely unknown product, startups have different challenges and priorities than well-established companies.

Nowhere is this more evident than when it comes to marketing and **PR**. While big name brands might have the luxury of dropping tens of thousands of dollars on major marketing and advertising campaigns, smaller companies just don't have that kind of budget.

Additionally, for startups, allocating funds toward marketing initiatives is often a gamble. As you have a relatively unproven product, you're often forced to make considerable assumptions about your target market, and then move forward with a strategy hoping for the best. If you're not careful, marketing can turn into a best-guess scenario pretty quickly, often resulting in wasted time and money.

Instead of shelling out for unproven efforts, startups would be better served by seeking out opportunities that offer the best bang for their buck.

One thing that's especially important for new companies is customer acquisition. For startups, looking for marketing initiatives that will support this goal should be a top priority. [1] (Chen)

As Sean Ellis, founder and CEO of GrowthHackers put it, "Marketing opportunities that offer a fast payback with additional profit margin are a key component for reaching your startup's full market potential." [2] (Ellis, 2012)

As a startup, it's imperative that you make your efforts count.

The beauty of PR is that it's very much a fluid process; one that lends itself perfectly to startups. It's something that can easily be molded to fit a company's needs and budget – no matter what its size. It can also be adjusted as you go, making it especially ideal for startups that are quickly growing and changing as they seek to stay competitive in a continually shifting global marketplace.

Best of all, it's something that gets results. It can get you noticed, put you on the map, and perhaps most importantly – draw in new customers. We've seen it work time and time again.

It's the 'how' and 'why' behind great media coverage that we've attempted to uncover in the book, in order to help you fast-track your efforts to secure the publicity that you so desperately need to stand out from the crowd.

Out of the Newsroom and Into Your Hands

Once upon a time, PR professionals relied heavily on traditional print media – newspapers and magazines, broadcasting – TV and radio, as well as direct mail and telemarketing to broadcast their messages.

Today, however, there's more to getting the word out than simply publishing a few articles in the Daily Herald. It's true that these forms of media are still in use, but today's PR is less about snail mail and more about generating information quickly and easily. Today's audience is tuned in and listening; and they want breaking news and stories.

How important PR is to your startup's marketing plan

Journalists, the gatekeepers to this audience, have changed as well. No longer are they the traditional newsroom publicists of the 20th century, printing yesterday's news. Most journalists have their finger firmly on the pulse of current events and are constantly looking for riveting stories and cutting-edge developments.

For startups today, it's easier than ever to get the word out about your new product and share your message with an engaged audience. Social media, custom email pitches, as well as Facebook and YouTube videos allow you to win over journalists and your audience alike and are excellent for facilitating the spread of information.

Being a startup in the information age, though, isn't without its share of difficulties. One of the main challenges is finding a way to stand out. When everyone has a platform, it can be difficult to be heard above all the noise. For this reason, you need a distinct strategy to differentiate yourself from the competition.

At its core, good PR relies on three distinct factors: conversation, a story, and connection – to distinguish a company from the crowd and to make a lasting impression.

How you can apply these three tools to your strategy and use them to expand your influence and reach is what we're going to look at now.

Conversation

Today, smart brands are beginning to shift their focus onto the lost art of the conversation.

While traditional advertising tactics rely primarily on one-way dialogue, and a brand shouting out their praises through a megaphone, brand endorsements from the companies themselves just don't cut it anymore.

Today's audience is a lot more savvy – and skeptical, and brand validation comes in the form of customer reviews, trusted sources, and even the occasional power user.

PR, at its heart, is a conversation. The best public relations strategies work to create two-way discussions and facilitate authentic dialogue with the audience.

A Story

How do you get the word out about your big idea, cool product, or announcement?

By telling a story.

While the idea of storytelling is a buzzword these days, the art of storytelling itself is timeless. Storytelling, at its finest, is about creating a narrative and painting a picture that your audience will not only comprehend, but also remember.

As Leo Widrich of Buffer explains, there's a fascinating process that takes place when we hear a story. Not only do the language-processing parts in the brain become activated, but so do the other areas of the brain that we would normally use when experiencing the events of the story ourselves. [3] (Widrich, 2012) We tend to relate to concepts and remember ideas better when we can experience those events ourselves, whether that's firsthand or through a story.

If you create a story that your audience can connect to, then they will certainly be interested in it.

One recent study found that 76% of journalists feel more pressure now to think about their story's potential to get shared on social platforms. [4] (Crimmons, 2016) Stories matter. And telling stories will always be key to an effective PR campaign.

The Connection

In addition to their love of stories and good conversation, people have a deep desire to connect.

This genuine connection is only becoming scarcer in the digital age, where, despite having hundreds of friends on social media, many people feel more disconnected than ever. [5] (Marche, 2012)

Effective PR involves creating stories and content that resonates and connects with people on a real level. Journalists, PR pros, and startups alike should be striving to form real connections with people, whether it's via visual and interactive media, such as YouTube, Facebook Live, and Instagram Stories, or through traditional print media. As PR continues to evolve and reinvent itself with the social age, creating a sharable community-based experience will increasingly become a top priority.

The best PR strategies today effectively weave conversations and stories. They're also designed to facilitate a connection between the brand and their audience. As a startup, you already have all of the elements that you need for a solid PR strategy. In the next few chapters we'll show you how you can unpack them, and start creating solid pitches that will help you to get the word out; allowing you to create stories that will not only be picked up by the media – but ones that will resonate with your audience as well.

To Do List:

It's time to brainstorm! This exercise is designed to get your creative wheels spinning.

- ☐ Ensure that you understand your startup's need for conversation, a story, and connections.
- ☐ Think about your startup's story. How could you tell it in a way that will engage your audience?
- ☐ Try to think of ways that you could use social media to connect with your audience.
- ☐ What conversations could you start?

CHAPTER 2

EXECUTING A WINNING PR STRATEGY: TWO CASE STUDIES

> *"Saying Hello doesn't have an ROI. It's about building relationships."*
> - GARY VAYNERCHUK

Over the years at our PR firm, Onboardly, whenever we would speak to a new client, one of our favorite questions to ask was, "What are your wish list media outlets? Which ones would you most like to be covered by?"

It may sound cheesy, but one of the perks of working in PR is that you can sometimes feel like a genie who grants wishes.

While many of our clients' dream outlets were just that, wishes, we had discovered there is value in setting your sights high. When the sky's the limit, you tend to have the most productive brainstorming sessions. Ultimately this led to some stellar PR initiatives as well.

The truth is, every founder and startup has their set of dream outlets, and choosing the right agency or partner can be the key to getting your messaging exactly where you want it to be.

But while it can be beneficial to think big, it's also important to begin your PR journey with a clear understanding of what, exactly, PR is and how it works.

How Does PR Work?

Whether you choose to hire a PR firm, or are planning to go it alone, it's important to have a clear understanding of PR and how it works.

At Onboardly, our clients would often come to us with unrealistic expectations. These were usually based on an unclear understanding of the PR process. We once had a client who, after two months of no media coverage, claimed to have only hired us for our 'media connections' and not our ability to craft the messaging and pitch the story to the right people at the right time; which is what a successful and long-term PR strategy is all about.

Despite many assumptions, having media 'connections' won't always come through for you. 'Calling in a favor' isn't as common as it once was either. Each media placement in a top-tier outlet takes a lot of work, every time. The fact is, journalists move around a lot and any PR agency that claims to have a connection with a top-tier publication based on a loose relationship with one writer there is treading on thin ice.

Good PR, first and foremost, is built on relationships; and those take time to cultivate. In fact, at Onboardly, we started building relationships years before we opened our doors.

A good PR agency will also work closely with you to polish your positioning and reach out to the press while your marketing side

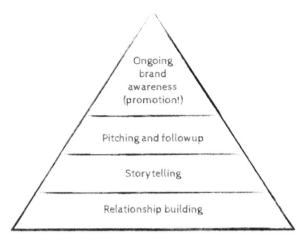

PR Hierarchy Pyramid

works on branding activities. They'll create a strategic approach that involves targeting the right journalists or publications, to increase the effectiveness of your campaigns; and improve your chances of both immediate and long-term success. With a great PR blitz, they'll kick start your marketing for you. [6] (Blank, 2006)

Finally, effective PR is also about timing and executing a strategy in a way that will generate publicity at key intervals.

To show you what we mean, let's take a look at two success stories from our years in PR. These case studies demonstrate the value of effective PR and also highlight the importance of relationship-building, strategy, and timing.

Case Study #1: Vendeve - The Business Network for Women Entrepreneurs

A few years ago, we were working on getting one of our clients into Forbes.

That client was Vendeve; a referral network for female entrepreneurs. When we started, we had a pretty good idea of the type of journalists that we needed to get to know to make it happen, and set to work looking for writers who covered female entrepreneurs and noteworthy startups.

But then we stumbled upon a Forbes contributor, Vanessa; a writer who frequently covered topics about family and finance. At first glance, this didn't exactly scream Vendeve, but with a little careful digging, we realized that it was a perfect fit. Vanessa was the type of person who was passionate about helping women. Or more specifically, helping women to achieve success, which is what Vendeve offered as well.

We immediately got to work getting to know Vanessa. To start, we began following her on Twitter. We could have sent an email introducing ourselves, but this was Forbes, the Holy Grail of business outlets, so we kept our cool and began this task slowly and gracefully.

We kept it for several weeks. The first week, we shared one of her recent articles on Twitter, commenting on how much we loved it. The second week we brought a broken link to her attention. From there, we continued to interact with her as we would anyone else we were following on Twitter.

As Women's Entrepreneurship Day rolled around that November, the timing was perfect. Vendeve got to work creating a 'Top 10 Tools for Female Entrepreneurs' post; something that we'd hoped Vanessa might be interested in covering.

By this point, we had tweeted enough with Vanessa to be comfortable shooting her a message asking if we could grab her email address and to see about getting in touch. When Vendeve's 'Top 10 Tools' post went live, we were ready to rock. We fired off the message, and within minutes we had received a response from her and a link to a contact form. We wasted no time in sending over our short-and-sweet pitch. By lunch that same day we had confirmed that Vanessa was interested in what we had to offer, and was ready to take the next steps to make things happen.

When we initially reached out to her, we had hoped that she would publish our list of tools, which of course included Vendeve, on November 19th - Women's Entrepreneurship Day. We were also optimistic that she might mention Vendeve's #WomenWOW pledge; where the company would be donating $1 to a Kiva entrepreneur for each sign-up that they received.

In the end, Vanessa did not publish our list of tools word for word, nor did she mention the pledge. The timing didn't quite work out either, and her story ran weeks after Women's Entrepreneurship Day.

Still, what Vanessa did do was even better than what we had planned. Vanessa ended up writing an entire piece on Vendeve, featuring some of their favorite tools created by women to help women. She also took the time to really get to know the founder of Vendeve, Katelyn Bourgoin. Instead of using some stock image, she used a real photo of Katelyn to complement the piece. And much to both Katelyn and Vendeve's surprise, she gave them one of the best compliments the young startup could have imagined:

"But the great thing about starting something like Vendeve as Facebook, LinkedIn and Yelp approach their adolescence is that it takes the best features from all of them and refines them."

Since being covered in Forbes, Vendeve noticed a massive spike in user sign-ups. Being able to namedrop recent Forbes coverage to investors was a bonus as well. The lesson here was not only that hard work pays off, but also that good things come to those who wait. Of course, it also highlights the importance of taking a relationship-based approach with PR.

The best media placements take time, and as Vendeve and so many of the other startups that we've worked with have come to realize, patience is everything.

What You Can Learn From Our Experience:

- Choose the journalist most likely to cover your story, and tell it well.
- When getting to know them, don't rush things. If journalists see that you follow them on Twitter, connect with them on LinkedIn, share their most recent content, and tweet or email them in the same 24 hours they'll sense an ulterior motive, and you probably won't get the coverage that you were hoping for.
- PR won't always go as planned, and that's okay. As long as your story isn't getting warped into negative PR, be open to change and trust your journalist. They know their outlet and their readers.

Case Study #2: Renters Warehouse - America's Fastest Growing Property Management Company

One time, a single press feature led to approximately half a million dollars in revenue for our client. In fact, the amount of traffic that poured in ended up crashing their website. We still chuckle about this today saying, "It was so good, we broke it."

That client was Renters Warehouse; one of America's largest and most-awarded property management companies. We had the pleasure of working with their in-house marketing department on social media, content marketing, and PR for over the course of three years. At the time, they were well-known in their home state of Minnesota, but they wanted to think bigger, sell more franchises, and dominate the U.S. market.

It's important to note that Renters Warehouse was doing incredibly well when they came to us. Their national growth was record-breaking, their company culture —award-winning, and they were rapidly expanding across the country. Despite being a phenomenal company, journalists weren't exactly jumping to cover them. If you listened carefully, you could hear the media saying, "Ok, so what?"

Enter founder and now-retired CEO Brenton Hayden. Brenton had a compelling backstory behind his foray to success. He had gone from being broke and getting evicted from his apartment, to building a successful property management empire. All before his 28th birthday.

A retired 28-year-old real estate millionaire with a heartfelt rags to riches story? There's your so what!

That's the kind of story that every 21-year-old entrepreneur, every budding real estate investor, and everyone who cries during America's Got Talent auditions wants to read. It was a story that was gripping enough to connect with an audience.

No one knew his story quite like Brenton himself, so we wanted him to be the one to tell it. We worked with him to write the story in a compelling way that would capture the attention of key publications and spark real discussion.

First, we narrowed in on what was truly unique about his story. Under 28? So is one-third of Silicon Valley. A millionaire? If you watch reality TV, you'll know that's not exactly newsworthy. What really stood out about Brenton's story is that he chose to retire at the height of his career. Once we had pinpointed the most interesting aspect of Brenton's story, it was time to move on to qualitative research.

We gathered a group of business-savvy entrepreneurs and told them Brenton's story individually, focusing on the fact that he was planning to retire. The response? Completely divided. Some said that it was crazy, irresponsible, and just plain stupid. Some said it was lazy and he'd get tired of those sandy beaches eventually. Others said it was ambitious and applauded his decision.

When we got these reactions, we knew that we were on the right track. Now that we knew how we were going to tell the story, we needed to decide where we wanted it published.

We ran through the top-tier business and tech publications and ultimately decided on Entrepreneur Magazine. It had a wide reach and lots of content partners; which would open us up to syndication opportunities. It also had a good mix of both experienced and inexperienced readers.

The piece went live in January. Almost immediately it began capturing attention. It would go on to be shared approximately 22,000 times and receive over 200 comments; not too shabby by Entrepreneur standards. On the day of publication, it was even picked up by Yahoo! Finance and quickly climbed to the first page, gaining even more views and attention.

The results:

- The piece had 500,000 views on Yahoo! and resulted in over 82,000 page views for Renters Warehouse. Approximately 16% of Yahoo! readers ended up on the Renters Warehouse website that same day.
- That month alone, Renters Warehouse saw 27% of the total page views they saw in the entire previous year.
- Renters Warehouse saw 23% more new visitors (vs. returning) during that same month.
- The month that the piece went live, Renters Warehouse's page views were 262.1% higher over the previous month.
- Renters Warehouse received more than 575 leads in the following two weeks. We estimate that would have been roughly $500,000 in revenue.

Extending Momentum

During the month following publication of the article, page views were still 122.8% higher, with no signs of slowing down. This is because we focused on extending momentum from the day we hit publish.

Here's what happened:

1. The Entrepreneur piece went live on January 27th.
2. The same day, it was picked up by Yahoo! Finance and made the first page via Entrepreneur's syndication network.
3. On January 31st, FOX News requested an interview with Brenton in NYC as a result of the Yahoo! Finance traction.
4. The Steve Harvey Show requested an interview with Brenton February 4th as a result of the Yahoo! Finance traction.
5. On February 5th, Business Insider ran the piece via Entrepreneur's syndication network.
6. Dozens of radio and podcast interview requests poured in. We had to turn down approximately 80% of these offers because the demand for Brenton's time was too high.
7. In October, we followed up with the Steve Harvey Show to see about having Brenton as a guest. The opportunity came to fruition on December 4th, almost a year after the initial Entrepreneur piece ran. We were especially excited about this opportunity because it would take Brenton out from behind a computer screen and put him into the spotlight where his charm could really shine. This would allow even more people to fall in love with his story.
8. On December 25th, Entrepreneur ran the piece a second time, resulting in just as much social media attention.

We often used the Entrepreneur and Yahoo! Finance pieces in our subsequent press outreach for Brenton and Renters Warehouse. It proved to be a great way to establish credibility and authority.

What You Can Learn From Our Experience:

- Crafting a story that's appealing and memorable can work for you time and time again.
- You don't always have to leave it up to the journalist to write your story.
- Always work with people who will help you to extend the momentum of every piece of coverage you get. We always connected with content partners, hit distribution networks, and stayed actively involved in industry social-bookmarking communities. PR isn't just about connecting with the media and journalists. It involves having a presence all over the internet.

A Word of Caution

While being picked up by the press is exciting, it's important to realize that a one-time feature isn't enough to secure your success. With PR, the best strategies are part of a continual, long-term plan that's designed to keep the news rolling, allowing you to continuously secure new coverage.

Your timing is also crucial, with each step of the process a careful balancing act. You need people to validate your idea, beta testers to test your product or service, and then a mass influx of customers to buy when it's ready to ship. How, when, and how strongly you execute a PR strategy is crucial to your success.

Act too soon, and you risk launching a product that's not ready or one that's unable to gain traction because it's had no validation.

Move too late, and someone else is already writing about it in a manner that may not be complimentary to your positioning.

When you control the message throughout the process the odds will tilt in your favor. A carefully executed and perfectly timed launch is vital for reaching your expectations and goals.

To Do List:

Timing is everything.

When it comes to PR, a common mistake is that the product isn't ready for the limelight. Take a moment to reflect on your product or idea. Where do you want your product to be when it gets the attention it deserves?

Take a moment to write down, not your minimal viable product, but the product that you would like to see featured in the media.

Your Ideal Product:

- [ ] What does it look like?
- [ ] Who is already covering it in the media?
- [ ] What celebrity is Instagraming or sharing videos about it?
- [ ] How many users does it have?
- [ ] What partnerships have you secured?
- [ ] Who is using it?
- [ ] If you have an API, who is using it?
- [ ] What integrations do you have?

CHAPTER 3

ARE YOU READY FOR PR?

"People do not buy goods and services. They buy relations, stories and magic."
- SETH GODIN

Are you ready for PR?

It seems like a silly question to ask, but you'd be surprised how many startups run straight to the press, without first assessing if they are ready for the impact that PR will have on their company. In our own experience, only about 15% of the approximately 200 startups that we spoke to over the course of a year were actually ready for publicity, although they think they needed it right then and there. Through several hundred phone calls and assessments, we determined that a startups' unpreparedness for PR very often came down to one of three things.

1) The Founder Has a Romanticized View of PR

It's not uncommon for founders to have a distorted view of PR. For some, it's all about that big media mention or seeing their picture on the cover of Fortune. For these founders, the idea of getting their company into the news seems exciting. Often, they believe that one big press feature or celebrity endorsement will set them up for life.

The concept of PR may sound glamorous, but if you don't have a clear understanding of what PR is, and how it works, you'll miss the mark. No amount of press will help your product or service to be successful if you haven't done the work to ensure that it's market-ready and positioned appropriately. A feature in TechCrunch is great, but it's not likely going to give you a loyal customer base for life. I've always said, "PR won't save a sh*tty product." Make sure you are ready for the media before you dive in.

2) The Founder's Wearing Rose-Colored Glasses

Unfortunately, many founders can only see the good when it comes to their startup. This is understandable, given that they've been devoted to their company for a while. Likewise, many startups feel that their product is disrupting the industry. But while disruptors may have accounted for 9% of the startups entering the market back in the 90s, today, industry disruptors are few and far between. [7] (Alexander, 2016),

It's important to have a clear and realistic perspective of your company before you get started with PR. As Tom Walsham, the Director of Product at The Working Group says, "Don't fall in love with your idea." [8] (Walsham, 2015) Fall in love with the problem instead. If you aren't realistic about your product or service, it can be quite the blow when your pitches begin to fall flat.

3) The Product's Not Ready

The third issue could be called 'The Chicken and the Egg Syndrome.' For startups, there are often many important conversations that need to take place, bugs to need to be fixed, and people that need to be hired before you are truly media ready. Here lies the syndrome: startups need traction to secure investor money, beta testers, more customers, or influential people to use their product. To gain these things, they often need press. On the other hand, though, it's important to ensure that you're not bringing your product to market too early; before it's truly ready. For this reason, startup founders should always ensure that they're clear on the purpose of PR, or, what exactly they're hoping to gain from the campaign.

At this point, you may have found that your startup is guilty of at least one of these issues. If so, don't worry, you're certainly not alone.

Our goal is to give you a realistic and accurate view of PR to help you avoid many common pitfalls that startups often fall victim to. We want to show you what you can do to get your product and company PR-ready, and then help you polish your image, refine your story, and put your best foot forward.

For this reason, we've developed a list of things you'll want to consider before you start reaching out to journalists.

Ready to get started? Here are the eight things that you should ensure before you pitch your product to the media.

1. Your Product Works As It Claims

This refers to products outside of beta testing. In our experience, only about 1-2% of beta products are media-ready immediately, and this 1-2% are usually exceptions in some way. Either they're being built by a team with a history of successful launches, backed by a giant corporation or investors, have a celebrity or well-known founder, or are quite literally game-changers.

When assessing this piece of the larger puzzle, make sure that you're telling yourself the whole truth about your product or service offering.

Here are some tips to ensure product readiness:

- Get rid of the bugs. Don't ignore issues or features that aren't working because they will not just 'work themselves out.'
- Ensure that your product's unique. Make sure that your product or service isn't an exact replica of something that already exists and is receiving a lot of media coverage. If it is, you'll need to work even harder to capture the attention of the media and their audience. Competition can be healthy, but you'll need to be extremely creative to cut through the clutter.
- Get a support team on standby. Ensure that you have a great team in place that is ready to fix any issues that might come from an influx of new users.

2. You've Established Key Messaging

What is key messaging? In a nutshell, it's your brand's story. It's a short and succinct elevator pitch for your company.

At this point, you'll want to fine-tune your messaging, and outline your key talking points. You'll also want to create a list of anecdotes that you can use to give quotes on the fly. Your company should also be firmly positioned, and you should know exactly where you stand in terms of industry trends and the competition. You should also have proof of your success with revenue and your client base; journalists want to see measurable results.

If you need some help with your key messaging, consider the following:
- It needs to be independently compelling and believable. You, your customers, and your company need to believe your message, and fully subscribe to what you're selling.
- It needs to articulate what you do, how you're different, and the value that you bring to your stakeholders. It must also differentiate you from your competition. If your message is already claimed by another company, it won't matter that it's compelling. If you aren't inherently unique, you'll need to dig a bit deeper to discover what sets you apart. With so many products and services competing for attention, you need to articulate something beyond how 'cool' yours is.

Here are two examples of companies who have perfected their key messaging:

Airbnb
- Airbnb lets you live like the locals. (Focus: The experience)
- Airbnb opens the doors to homes around the world. (Focus: Access)
- Airbnb inspires a richer travel experience. (Focus: Optimizing travel)

Uber
- Everyone's private driver. (Focus: The feeling of luxury)
- Uber is an app that provides you with the simplest and most

reliable taxi service around. (Focus: Quick access)

Another great example of a company that has their messaging on point is Up Sonder, a startup that we had the pleasure of working with at Onboardly. Up Sonder is the first on-demand drone rental marketplace.

Take a look at that messaging: *Up Sonder is the first on-demand drone rental marketplace.* Boom! You read one sentence, you immediately know what they're offering. It sounds exciting too.

If you can't nail your messaging, you're not ready for the media. Put as much time, attention, and even reflection into your company's message as you can. It doesn't have to be long, but it needs to be powerful. It matters.

3. You've Created Your Positioning Statement

A positioning statement is an expression of how a product, service or brand fills a particular consumer's needs in a way that its competitors do not. In other words, it's a concise description of your target market as well as a compelling picture of how you want that market to perceive your brand.

Positioning statements help to bring clarity, focus, and direction to your marketing strategy. They leverage your expertise to help grow your startup, while also defining your marketing tactics. Perhaps most importantly, they give you a frame of reference from which to make decisions about your image; just like your brand name and its essence.

Unfortunately, the traditional model for writing an effective positioning statement is stale.

It goes something like this:

> For [insert Target Market], the [insert Brand] is the [insert Point of Differentiation] among all [insert Frame of Reference] because [insert Reason to Believe].

Boring, right? Times have changed, and so has the average positioning statement. If you're unclear about your positioning statement, here are some questions to help guide you:

What Is It?

This simply states what your company does. This is not about describing the value of your product or service, or why it's different from other things, so keep it very short and use plain English.

What's Your Market Segment?

This is the description of the target customers your startup is going after right now. The trick here is to focus on who you will sell to over the next six months, not your broader, ultimate market. These are the customers that you are most likely to close in the short-term.

Which Market Category Will You Compete In?

Now, zoom in a bit closer. Startups often have a choice of multiple categories that they could compete in. Narrowing in will help you to identify what the real competitive alternatives will be.

What Are Your Competitive Alternatives?

What other companies or solutions are competing with you?

Take the customer's perspective into account and include things that aren't necessarily direct competitors such as 'hiring an intern' or even 'doing nothing.'

For Onboardly, our competitors weren't just other PR agencies, but were also in-house marketing teams and publicists as well. Think broadly about who you are really competing against as it may not be immediately obvious.

What Key Benefit Does Your Product or Service Offer?

This is the single biggest benefit that your target buyer gains by using your product or service offering. Think about the one thing you would tell your customers about if you only talk about one single benefit.

What Is Your Primary Differentiation?

Finally, what is it that sets your product or service apart?

4. You Can Prove That You're Different

Next, you'll want to prove that you're different. Or, to put it another way, you'll need show prospective customers why you are. Here are some questions that will help you to demonstrate your product's uniqueness:

- Does your product or service have any unique bells or whistles that can show rather than tell?
- What anecdotes can you share with the press that will support the claims you're making?
- Do you have a story about how your product or service has changed someone's life?

Think about every customer touchpoint as a piece of the PR

puzzle. One well-crafted and articulated story can catapult your business forward, as we've seen with the earlier Renters Warehouse example. Being able to demonstrate that you're different will solidify whether you're newsworthy or not.

5. You Have a Company Spokesperson

Another important component to media readiness is having a company spokesperson. Ideally, they should be confident, a decision maker, authentic, available, and ready to rock.

Confident

First of all, your spokesperson should be a confident speaker. They should know your story, the problem your product or service solves, the marketplace, and trends inside and out.

A Key Decision Maker

The media typically wants to talk to the founder. For larger companies with an executive team (once your startup eventually gets there), they could also speak with a well-known corporate spokesperson.

Authentic

Your spokesperson needs to be likable, trustworthy, and someone that others admire.

Available

Your spokesperson must also be available. Free to take phone calls, answer emails and get interviewed. In our own experience, there have been many times we have had to back out of some exciting media opportunities because the company spokesperson wasn't there when we needed them. Often during launch, announcements, and other campaigns, it's best to make sure your spokesperson's schedule is clear of too many meetings, travel, or other engagements that may take them away from meeting the press.

Ready to Rock

Ideally, the spokesperson you've chosen for your company will have had some media training or experience and is ready for the spotlight. At the very least, they should be an excellent storyteller who's genuinely excited to talk about your startup.

6. You Have a Defined Audience

Before you can embark on a PR campaign, you should first know exactly who you are targeting, and why. Whether it's one segment or a dozen, you must know where your ideal customers are hanging out and have an idea of how they can be reached. You should also know what publications your users are reading, in order to focus on outlets that you know will actually convert.

7. You're Okay With Exclusivity

Most reporters and journalists want to feel special; like they are the only person who's had the privilege of hearing about your startup. With this, you recognize that you may have to throw out an embargo or offer exclusivity to a select publication. Understandably, most startups want all of the top publications to mention or feature their new product, but the fact is that it rarely works that way.

Unless you are launching something that's guaranteed to

change the world, are a recognized founder with a track record, or you have proven customer traction, you may have to settle for exclusivity, and that's okay. You can still get media attention from other outlets later on.

8. You're Willing to Invest Time and Money

Are you willing to invest the time and money that comprehensive PR requires? A solid budget for a startup will usually run between USD $3,000 - $15,000 per month depending on the PR professional or firm that you hire. If you decide to do it yourself, make sure you're able to commit the time to uphold the demanding schedule.

9. You Have Realistic Expectations

One final key to being media ready is having realistic expectations. There is no silver bullet in PR, and often it's partly cloudy with a 20% chance of rain. There is no perfect answer and nothing is guaranteed. If you're searching for that in PR, you'd be wise to shop elsewhere. Outcomes in PR exist on a continuum, and you have to buy in on the whole process. It takes time to build and support an effective campaign, but when it's good, it's really good.

Here is where those realistic expectations come into play again: just because you turn on the PR hose doesn't mean that big coverage will begin immediately. It can take two months, or longer, to start seeing media hits, so plan your product or service launches accordingly. Make sure you give yourself enough time to formulate a comprehensive strategy.

Taking the time to ensure that you're ready for what's ahead will allow you to lay a solid foundation; increasing your chances of PR success, and ensuring that you're not wasting time or money on a premature campaign.

Start by making sure your product or service works the way you claim it does. Get clear on your key messaging and positioning. Be ready to prove that you're different from the hundreds of other startups out there competing for the attention of the world. Have a spokesperson who is ready and willing to handle the spotlight. Know exactly who your target audience is. Possess the foresight to be okay with exclusivity in your PR efforts. Be willing to invest the time and money necessary for comprehensive PR, and be realistic, because as is the case with everything as a startup, nothing is ever guaranteed.

To Do List:

Are you ready for PR?

Fight the urge to jump to the next chapter and go through our list before deciding to pitch your product to the media. Once you can check off each item, you'll be able to ensure that you've laid the groundwork necessary for campaign success.

Here is your checklist for ensuring PR readiness:

- [ ] Your product works (As advertised).
- [ ] You've established key messaging.
- [ ] You've created your positioning statement.
- [ ] You can prove that you're different.
- [ ] You have a company spokesperson.
- [ ] You have a defined audience.
- [ ] You're okay with exclusivity.
- [ ] You're willing to invest time and money.
- [ ] You have realistic expectations.

CHAPTER 4

CRAFTING THE ULTIMATE STORY

> *"A good PR story is infinitely more effective than a front-page ad."*
> - SIR RICHARD BRANSON

No matter how wonderful your product or service is, it will never build a community of loyal supporters simply by existing. We live in an age where people believe that the products and services we buy say something about who we are.

Without a story, it will be difficult to assign meaning to your campaign, and even more challenging to persuade someone to subscribe to your product. We live in the age of identity, and identity is all about the narrative we're telling.

Storytelling gurus like Lisa Cron remind us that human beings are hardwired to respond to stories. [9] (Cron, 2013) It comes as no surprise then, that using effective storytelling in your marketing can have a major effect on the behavior of your customers. Psychology Today supports the argument in saying that "[Functional] MRI neuro-imagery shows that, when evaluating brands, consumers primarily use emotions (personal feeling and experiences) rather than information (brand attributes, features and facts)." [10] (Murray, P.N., 2013)

At the end of the day, your customers won't be buying your product or service; they'll be buying into your story because of the emotional response it triggers in them. If you can make someone feel that your story is about them, or somehow appeal to their values or beliefs then you'll have their attention.

Many founders find themselves wondering if their startup even has a story. The truth is, it almost certainly does! It may take some digging to uncover your narrative, but it's worth spending some time to get this right. It may not be easy, but narrative is one of the most vital pieces for attracting an audience, getting your company noticed, and securing the press coverage that you deserve.

In telling your story, you have the opportunity to show your company to the world. Too many businesses 'dress to impress' when really, truth and vulnerability are what's needed most.

Your startup story, who you really are, is what will resonate with your audience.

Finding Your Story

> *"If a story is not about the hearer he will not listen. And here I make a rule - a great and interesting story is about everyone or it will not last."*
>
> - JOHN STEINBECK, East of Eden.

As a startup, your narrative is your ultimate secret weapon, even if you don't quite know what it is yet.

To help you find your story, we've created 'The 5 Question Exercise.' Use these questions as a framework for writing your story.

- What inspired you/your team to start your company?
- Why are you, or your company, so amazing?
- Why is your product or service relevant now?
- What do you stand for?
- How is your company changing the world?

Take a moment to actually put your responses in writing. Getting clear on what sets you apart from similar companies will give you a solid foundation to craft your story.

As you begin to write, it is important to keep a few things in mind: your audience, your purpose, and your unique offering. Let's look at each of these in turn.

Your Audience

In a paradoxical way, your story should both take its shape from, and cater to your audience. Just like your product or service, your story is not a one-size-fits-all production. Your audience is not, nor should it be everyone, and having a targeted narrative will help you reach the right people. If you craft it correctly, your story will only speak to the audience that it was designed for.

Developing some customer personas can help you to think about your audience in a more personal way, allowing you to get inside the mind of your consumer to better understand the reasoning behind their purchasing decisions and helping you to craft your story in a way that will connect with them.

Customer personas are specific examples of people in your target market. We recommend that you try to create three to five such personas, in order to incorporate the bulk of your audience.

Not sure what to include? Consider the following:

- Their name and gender
- Their location
- Their profession, and salary
- Their family situation (married, kids, etc.)
- Their goals and the challenges they face
- Their values and fears

This is a great opportunity for you to include some details that you already know about your target audience and direct quotes from your customers. You can find these details with a bit of sleuthing. Start by looking for data in your site analytics, do some research on social media, or poll your audience. [11] (Lee, 2015)

Your Purpose

Next, getting clear on the central problem that your product or service solves will give you the 'purpose' of your startup story. Start by developing a list of the pain-points that your customer has, and outline how your product or service solves them. [12] (Points, 2011) From there, zero in on the most important problem to focus on; the one that matters most to your target audience.

Your Unique Offering

You may not be the only startup with that particular purpose and audience but you are the only startup that can solve it in the way you do. Make the case for why you are the best company to do so. Finding your unique selling position is essential to your success. It is quite literally, what your company stands for. [13] (Putnam, 2012)

Creating Your Story

Now that you've nailed the key elements necessary for your story, it's time to make it memorable.

Here are some characteristics that every engaging story should have:

- **Honesty**: Your narrative needs to be genuine in order to connect with your audience. Vulnerability is key, and being open about your mistakes or any hurdles that you faced will show that you're human. Far from alienating your audience, this level of honesty will draw them in.
- **Simplicity**: Good stories are only as long as necessary. The length of yours is irrelevant as long as you're saying everything that you need to in a clear and concise way. Be ruthless with your editing, anything that's included should be there for a reason.
- **Emotional Complexity**: Your narrative should be easy to understand, but that doesn't mean it should be superficial. Reflect the complexity of life by putting a focus on the nuances of its players. Never insult your reader's intelligence with simple dichotomies; life is rarely black and white. Instead, go the extra mile to ensure that your story paints a true picture of startup life.
- **Credibility**: Good stories are not built on laundry lists of figures and graphs, but good research can appeal to emotion. Presenting your research findings in a meaningful way increases both your credibility and trustworthiness. [14] (Rush, 2014)
- **Intrigue**: We stop watching a basketball game when our team is winning by a longshot because we already know the ending. Using basic intrigue tactics is a great way to keep your audience engaged.

- **Subtlety**: It is natural to want to control the outcome of your story for your audience, but you shouldn't. Following the old 'show don't tell' rule can help you make a powerful emotional impression. As marketing guru and bestselling author Seth Godin says, your story will be that much more convincing and believable when you allow your audience to come to the conclusion best supporting their worldview. [15] (Godin, 2006)
- **Speed**: You don't have a lot of time to win your audience over. Creating a strong first impression is imperative. In his bestselling book Blink, Malcolm Gladwell argues that people subconsciously "thin slice" situations within a matter of seconds. [16] (Gladwell, 2007) That means that for better or worse your audience will make a decision about you almost immediately.
- **Tone**: Ensure that there is synergy between the tone of your story, your brand, and your message. If you are unsure of what tone to take; test! Create multiple versions of your narrative and test which gets the most meaningful reactions for you. It's all about navigating the expectations of your audience.

When you're confident that your story includes these characteristics you can then add in the elements essential for a successful startup story.

Writing a Successful Startup Story

There are many elements that can be woven together to create a good story, but a good startup story requires characters with depth, context for conflict, and a satisfying ending that signals a change.

- **Characters With Depth**

  Investing the time to give your characters (founder/s, team, customers) some dimension is key to a successful startup story. Go beyond the basic facts and incorporate what you've learned from creating your client personas. You need to create characters so believable that your audience can't help but identify with their problems and decisions.

A great example of this was the 'Zappos Family Culture Blog.' The wildly successful online shoe retailer created a section of their blog solely dedicated to fun profiles of their employees; who they are, what they like to do, and how their values serve the customers. Characterizing all of the people who work for them and not just high-level executives allowed them to connect with their customers in a more meaningful way.

- Context for Conflict

    Developing the plot or setting for your conflict will make it more meaningful for your audience. The setting is the mood or backdrop of your narrative, while the plot works to drive the story forward. Both help to add some much-needed context and are key to helping your audience understand the problem that your company solves for them. It doesn't have to be a dark and brooding tale; comedies are an excellent example of incidents explored through a humorous lens.

- A Satisfying Ending That Signals a Change

    Think of your story as following the classic 'storytelling arc' with conflict at the peak. Consider how your characters (founder/s, team, customers) have grown or changed since the problem was expressed. A believable change in character will compel your audience to take action. Give them something inspiring.

For a masterful example of storytelling, let's break down the story of startup 15Five.

The story begins when North Face and ESPRIT founder Doug

Tompkins developed a system for streamlining employee feedback. His system? To have his employees spend fifteen minutes writing a report; one that would take him no more than five minutes to read. The idea was such a success within his own company that he decided to share it with his friend, Patagonia founder Yvon Chouinard who in turn told Sundia's CEO, Brad Oberwager. Unfortunately, though, Oberwager experienced issues when he tried to implement this system in his 100+ employee business. Not surprisingly, he simply couldn't keep up with that many reports.

At this point in the story, the main characters and the problem are becoming clear

Next, we see the context for conflict. Because Oberwager was having trouble implementing the idea, he decided to turn the practice into a software program; one that he would go on to share with David Hassell. Hassel had the vision to take things to the next level. He found a way to turn the reports into conversations and eventually, the resulting product, 15Five was formed. Hassell's change allowed 15Five to become the reason that thousands of employees in a range of businesses feel valued, supported, and free to address their concerns.

Finally, we arrive at a satisfying ending signalling change.

15Five transitioned from a simple practice that one man was using, to a movement that is truly changing the lives of working people all over North America. [17] (15Five)

While your story won't be the same as 15Five's, if you can craft it in a way that will include characters with depth, context for development, and a satisfying ending signalling chance, you'll be well on your way toward creating your own compelling story.

Now, let's look at some things you'll want to avoid when crafting your startup story.

Mistakes to Avoid:

1. Creating a Sales Pitch

Please don't think of your company story as a sales pitch. If you're trying to push something through your story, a journalist will be able to spot it a mile away. Instead, look to provide something that's worth publishing, and avoid the hard-sells.

2. Knocking the Competition

The story that centres around why your product is better than the competition's will get you nowhere fast. No one wants to read yet another story of why your company is doing so much better than company X. Make sure your story brings something real to the table; and doesn't just knock down the competition.

3. Overwhelming With Facts and Figures

A company story that's jam-packed with nothing but facts, figures, and important dates is likely to be of importance to nobody but you. Keep your story lively with exciting and meaningful milestones that will capture the attention of an audience.

4. Talking About Yourself Too Much

Above all, avoid stories that are solely about you, and not your customer. If you don't craft your narrative with your customer in mind, it will never resonate with them. We buy from companies that we feel understand our needs. When you put your customer at the heart of your story, you'll be able to create something that they'll want to listen to.

Getting Your Story Out Into the World

"The best product doesn't always win. The best entrepreneur does."
- TONY ROBBINS

It's tempting to think that all you need is a good product. But while the quality of your product or service is an essential component for long-term success, it is the combination of a good product and a winning story that separates the everyday brands from the great ones.

Marketers are no strangers to storytelling and often leverage it to their advantage. This results in the online space being bombarded with roughly 5.3 trillion ads per year [18] (Read, 2016) and over 2 million blog posts published every day. [19] (Puranjay, 2015)

In a sea of endless options, you need a way to ensure that your story stands out.

The truth is, one news story will not set you up for life. Very few people will remember your company after hearing about you once. But, don't let this discourage you. Every time a potential customer hears about you, it helps to build awareness. Many marketing experts believe that Dr. Jeffrey Lant's 'Rule of 7' applies here. This rule states that in order to penetrate your potential buyer's consciousness as well as create a significant impact in your market, you have to make contact a minimum of seven times over an 18-month period. [20] (Business Insider, 2011). This means that you need to find ways to continually keep your business in the public eye.

How can you do that?

One way is to systemize for success. Consider keeping a 12-month calendar for your press outreach. Begin filling it in with the obvious things, such as funding announcements. From there, you and your team can fill in any blank spots with creative ideas to take to the press. Keep seasonality and timely events in mind as you fill up your calendar. PR sprints are generally six to eight-week cycles, but that may be too long for your company; refresh your angles, story, and approach every month or two. Work on improving as you move forward and iterating as you learn.

At the end of the day, products come and go, but a good story has staying power. And as you'll see as you go along, it will continually form the base of your PR strategies and campaigns going forward.

To Do List:

It's time to tell your story!

Close your book, sit down, and close your eyes. Get comfortable.

Now reflect on your story and answer the following questions:

- [ ] What inspired you/your team to start your company?
- [ ] Why are you, or your company, so amazing?
- [ ] Why is your product or service relevant now?
- [ ] What do you stand for?
- [ ] How is your company changing the world?

Once you've reflected on these questions, it's time to put your responses in writing. You can then use these answers to help guide your story.

You will need two different stories: a founder story and a start-up story. Explain why there is a need for your startup and why you were the person (the expert) to bring it to market. Did you solve your own problem? Did you see a gap in the market? Was it a discovery, or an experiment? Jot down your notes and begin crafting your story.

CHAPTER 5

THE PRESS RELEASE. WHY IT STILL EXISTS AND HOW TO USE IT

"Publicity is the act of getting ink. Publicity is getting unpaid media to pay attention, write you up, point to you, run a picture, make a commotion. Sometimes publicity is helpful, and good publicity is always good for your ego."
- SETH GODIN

Ah, the press release.

One of the words most commonly associated with the idea of public relations. Its importance and relevance, now in a digital era, commonly questioned.

While many startups might feel that the press release is an outdated concept and no longer necessary, the fact is there are many benefits to having one.

Though its formatting and style have certainly changed since the early days of public relations, one thing remains the same: the press release continues to be one of the most common and effective ways to share company news with both the digital and traditional media world. And while a press release will never replace a thoughtful, well-written pitch to a journalist, it does one heck of a job complementing it.

In its most basic form, a press release can contain anything newsworthy about your company.

Examples of news that could merit a press release:

- A funding announcement
- A product or new feature launch
- The appointment of a new CEO or executive
- An event, charity, or community involvement
- A merger or acquisition

A press release provides journalists with the details (the who, what, when, where, why) about your news. It's a rundown on the facts, and when done properly, it gives the press everything they need to write a great story about your company and its announcement.

When it comes to writing your press release, you'll want to think like a journalist. One common misconception is that press releases are dry and boring, but they don't have to be.

Think about how you read the news, and the stories you gravitate towards. For most of us, It's usually news that elicits some type of emotional response, whether that's excitement, fear, or sadness. This doesn't mean that you should make people cry, but your press release should get people excited. Be interesting, be colorful, and have fun writing it. Give the press no choice but to tell your story.

The Purpose of the Press Release

If you're planning to handle your own PR, you'll want to learn how to leverage a press release.

But first, let's take a look at what a press release can and can't do.

A press release will not do all the work that a good publicist can. It doesn't matter how perfectly written your press release is. Simply writing it and sending it to your target media list will not turn your news into feature stories. Relationships AND a press release will do this.

A well-written press release can mean the difference between a writer finding time for your story or passing on it all together. It's no secret that journalists today are often strapped for time. Many media outlets are operating understaffed and journalists are frequently so busy working on their assignments that their hands are often tied even if they want to help you with your announcement.

To a journalist who's pressed for time, a well-written pitch and detailed press release can mean the difference between yes and no. Think about it. If you only hint at your news in your pitch or provide a few high-level bullet points, the journalist will likely require more info and may have to book a call with you in order to learn more. They may not have time for that. But by providing a press release that includes everything they need, you'll cut their workload in half. If they're especially busy, they may even choose to run your press release as it is; as long as you've done a good job at telling your story in the release, that is.

A press release can get attention days, months, or years later. One of the things we love most about the press release is their staying power. While their spotlight on the newswire will be short-lived, if you house your press releases on your website's press page, visitors to your site will be able to see past news for years to come. Google will continue to pull up your press releases when people search for your startup, which is excellent for SEO.

The Newswire

The newswire is a service that transmits the latest news stories; gathering reports and selling them to subscribing news organizations.

The word dates back to the days of the telegraph, referring to the wires that were used to transmit information. Today, the newswire still provides up-to-date information to the media about breaking news and events.

Newswires are made up of journalists and editors who cover news stories for a particular company, and they represent an official source of information for them. Luckily, you don't have to have a PR professional on your team to make use of these valuable services.

But first things first: should you use the newswire or not?

This is entirely up to you. It's one of the only press release distribution methods that has a price tag associated with it, which can make it an immediate 'heck no' for many. While there are various press release platforms to choose from, most will come with a price tag of anywhere from $150 to $500 to distribute your release.

For some startups, that may simply be out of the budget, and that's okay. There are other ways to distribute your release for free.

But what if the newswire is in your budget?

Here's how you can get started:

1. **Sign up for an account.** Register with the newswire service of your choice (we love Cision's PR portal). Do this before you're ready to launch your first press release, as it can take up to 24 hours for your account to be approved.

2. **Get to know your account manager.** We can't stress this one enough. We realize that time is precious and you may not want to spend a half an hour getting a product demo, but if it's your first time using a newswire platform, it's totally worth it. They will take the time to understand your goals, your company, and share with you the most effective way for you to get your newswire distributed. Make time for these calls! You'll thank us later.

3. **Get clear on the cost.** Signing up for an account is often free, but there are usually fees associated with posting your releases. Some newswires charge by the word, for a certain number of words, or may give you several flat fee options to choose from. Depending on the urgency of your release, as well as any extra bells and whistles you choose to add, you will generally be looking at a cost of about $250 to $450 per release. Some newswires offer bundle deals that can help reduce costs, which are a good idea if you're planning to distribute regularly.

4. **Schedule your release(s).** Once your account is approved, the newswire service will walk you through the process. You'll be able to choose when and where you want your information to be released, and will also be able to target certain geographical regions and industries based on categories. At Onboardly, we found that Tuesdays, Wednesdays, and Thursdays were the best days to publish releases for our clients. On Monday, journalists are busy digging through their inboxes, and by Friday they're usually finish-

ing up their stories for the week and aren't looking for more. We've found that 7 a.m. EST is a great time to schedule releases for publication.

5. **Be mindful of other parties involved.** If you're distributing news strictly on behalf of your company, you should receive an approval quite quickly, but if you're mentioning other companies or people, you may require their authorization. This is often the case with news of major partnerships or acquisitions.

6. **Check in on your releases.** Once your press release is out on the wire you can use your account to check in on what media outlets are picking up your information. Be aware, however, that you can have any number of pick-ups and still no one writing anything of substance about your startup. Many times you'll find that outlets may just re-publish your release verbatim. Do a quick Google search for your startup to see which journalists are actually writing about you.

Your press releases will always be distributed with your contact information included, so whenever you're distributing a release, ensure that your phone is handy in case the media calls. Just be aware that this can be a bit of a double-edged sword. You're giving journalists the opportunity to speak to you or your founder directly, which is excellent; but at the same time, you're also opening yourself up to people you may not be interested in talking to, who might try to sell you things like other press release services or media monitoring tools. Don't let that deter you, though, the newswire is still a fantastic way to get your news out to the world.

Other Things to Do With Your Press Release

For some companies, simply allowing their newswire to be picked up organically and show up in search engine results is all they need or want. But you can do so much better than that. If you want to get the best results, your work doesn't end there.

- **Send It to the Media**

  With thousands of companies distributing news on the newswire, don't rely on it to secure you praiseworthy media. If you want your local newspaper or your favorite digital outlets to pick up your story, make it easy for them to do so by sending your press release their way.

  Better yet, send your press release to any news outlet that you'd like to have cover your news under embargo ahead of your announcement date. Give them plenty of time to interview you or relevant parties for the article and write a great article you can be proud of. And remember, no journalist wants to get a press release the night before you expect them to write about it.

- **Display It on Your Website or Blog**

  If you've put effort into writing a press release, why not leverage it as valuable content? Publish it on your company blog or add it to your website's press page. If you don't have one, get one set up. This will look great down the road when potential customers, investors, or curious folks check out your webpage to learn more about your history and success.

- **Distribute It to Your Mailing List or Team**

  Got a mailing list? You have a world-class distribution channel. If your press release is relevant to your customers or subscribers, include it in your company newsletter. Celebrate your success with your entire team by sharing your press release internally to your team and stakeholders.

Once you've had some experience writing press releases and distributing them to the media, you'll realize how seamlessly you can build them into your overall communications strategy. Depending on the size of your company and how often you have news or hit milestones, you may be able to distribute anywhere from one release per week or month to one every quarter.

You won't get picked up by journalists every time, but getting your company news out there will pay off in more ways than one.

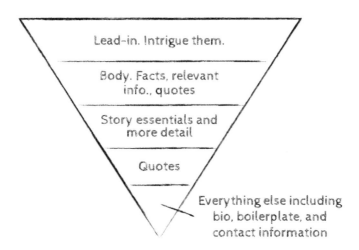

The Press Release Pyramid

The To Do List:

Are you ready to write your first press release?

Close your eyes and think of what exciting newsworthy things will be happening at your company over the coming months. Are there any events that you could orchestrate? Perhaps volunteering for a charity event? Or renting a booth at an upcoming expo?

- ☐ Start writing down upcoming milestones.
- ☐ If you have nothing planned, brainstorm and jot down potential events that you could orchestrate.
- ☐ Mark your calendar so that you can remember to create a press release to publish following the event.
- ☐ Determine how you will share it with the media, your customers, and your stakeholders.

CHAPTER 6

ESTABLISHING GOALS AND TRACKING YOUR PR EFFORTS

> *"Not everything that can be counted counts, and not everything that counts can be counted."*
> - BRUCE WILLIAM CAMERON

Not all coverage is created equal!

But how can you tell when your efforts are paying off? How do you know when you're getting results and when you're just firing off pitches into a black hole?

Gaining an understanding of the value of press coverage and mentions is incredibly important for startups. PR is all about listening carefully and telling stories to reach your target audience. When you're able to measure it properly, you'll be able to determine quickly what's working and what isn't. [21] (AirPR)

Perhaps no one puts it better than CEO and co-founder of Air-

PR Sharam Fouladgar-Mercer. According to Fouladgar-Mercer, "Before the advent of PRTech began to enable dot-connecting between PR activities and business goals, PR professionals had to rely on gut instinct and subjective rationale for all decision making. Now, because PR is finally getting access to data and tech, PR professionals can use that data to identify which outlets, journalists, and story types can deliver real results for their business (traffic back to site, message pull through, etc.)."

Fouladgar-Mercer goes on to say that data creates an objective feedback loop and represents a crucial component for optimization. He also maintains that both ego and personal bias need to be removed from the equation in order to determine where a company's efforts are best invested.

So how can you measure the impact that PR has on your company?

To begin, let's consider the power of earned media. It may surprise you to learn that your press mentions, reviews, and endorsements are trusted far more than traditional advertising. [22] (Neilson, 2015) Not only that but earned media increases the overall trust your audience has in your startup as well.

Mentions can come from almost anywhere, resulting in an enormous amount of data for you and your team to sift through. The process of sorting through everything can be arduous, but it's necessary if you want to reveal the consumer patterns, trends, and associations that are so critical to a successful PR strategy. [23] (Trendkite)

Establishing Realistic Metrics

Not long ago, companies would have to wait for an entire year to learn the effectiveness of their PR campaigns.

Fortunately, we live in an age where that wait time has decreased significantly: the success (or failure) of your campaigns can now be determined almost immediately. Even so, Christine Perkett, founder, and SEO of PR metrics company SeeDepth mentions that there's always the risk of denial. "Too many PR folks don't want to admit that something's not working," Perkett says. "But when the needle isn't moving as promised, it's obvious."

With so much riding on your ability to see what's working for your startup, you need to consider a few things before jumping in.

1. Identify Your Goal

Knowing what you want to accomplish is the first step. Are you looking for more leads? Improved margins? More fundraising? Whatever your goal may be, ensuring that you're clear about it before you begin trying to measure your PR will help you make sure that every step you take is in pursuit of it.

Make sure that your goals are specific, and that they take into account the following:

- **Reach:** What part of your target audience do you want to reach, and with what messaging?
- **Awareness:** What new things should your target audience see, hear, or read?
- **Comprehension:** What should your target audience understand that they didn't before?
- **Attitude:** What should your target audience feel and believe?
- **Behavior:** What should your audience do as a result of your messaging? [24] (Ketchum)

2. Make Sure Your Campaigns Support Your End Goal

It may seem obvious, but designing your PR campaigns with your end goal in mind is incredibly important. During a campaign, you 'go live' with your plan of action which includes press releases, news stories, and more, so you'll want to ensure that each piece supports your goal.

3. Monitor Your Campaign

Attempting to work backward once a campaign has ended can result in missed opportunities and frustration for you and your team. Using a tool like Google Alerts, though, can help you observe the interactions that your customers are having with your brand, campaigns, and marketing strategies as they occur. According to a white paper by Ketchum Global Research and Analytics, startups should look for issues they may want to react to, identify trends in the opinions of their consumers, and take a qualitative analysis of their content. [25] (Ketchum)

4. Measure Your Success

There is no more concrete way to prove that your campaign was a success than having the data to back it up. Log your data into a spreadsheet as it comes in to help your team connect the dots more quickly later on. Work to quantify your reach and tone, identify the top consumers of your messaging, and make benchmarks in advance of activity so that you can track changes over time. [26] (Ketchum)

Choosing your goal is the first step, but now you need to figure out the best metrics and performance indicators to watch for while your campaigns are in action.

What Should You Measure?

Metrics are industry, company, and campaign-specific.

No matter what way you choose to measure success, you can

learn something from every pitch email, media mention, and fan interaction. The right metrics combined with a clear goal should indicate the tactics that your startup should continue using, which things you should add in, and where you should make strategic cuts. [27] (AirPR)

In our own broad internal assessment at Onboardly, we would keep track of hours spent on pitches versus their success in the media. We'd look at how much time and energy it took to get a journalist to say 'yes.' Doing this helped us to understand the amount of time (read: money) that we were investing in each opportunity, and also demonstrated our conversion rate.

Externally, we needed to determine the value that each media mention, feature, or story brought to our clients. We began by analyzing the traffic these stories were bringing to our clients' websites and the probable bump we were gaining in SEO. We also looked at general awareness, or, how many people would see/read the article over its lifespan, as well as new customer acquisition.

These metrics are what we determined would work for us. While all were weighted differently, each played an important role in assigning value.

Each startup is different, and our performance indicators may not be applicable to your company. However, there are a few things that we recommend you start tracking today to gain some valuable insights on your campaigns.

1. Interactions With Your Pitch

Monitoring each interaction with your pitch will help you to identify which of your messages are resonating with your audience, and which ones are falling flat. When looking at interactions, consider sentiment (the general feeling that customers, prospects, and the general public have of your brand) as well as target audience effects (the actions your audience takes after engaging with your campaign). [28] (Trendkite) Use this information as a learning opportunity, and to refine your pitches over time.

Some important questions to ask yourself while examining your interactions are:

- How many people received the email, opened it, forwarded it to colleagues, and clicked on the link?
- How many contacts replied, asking for more information?
- After posting on social media, how many fans/followers replied, clicked, retweeted, and shared? [29] (Pr Daily, 2014)

Tools like YesWare and MailChimp can help you track open rates and other important metrics, and it's worth spending some time familiarizing yourself with tools that will help to give you the data that you need.

2. Coverage of Your Outreach

Be aware of all coverage of your social media, web, and print outreach. It's a great idea to keep track of the different publication tiers, or types of publications that your startup is being mentioned in. [30] (Trendkite)

Some questions you should ask yourself about your outreach include:

- How many people are talking about my news?
- Who are the people talking about my startup, and how influential are they?
- What medium is talking about my startup, and how popular is it? [31] (Pr Daily, 2014)

This aspect of measurement requires a bit more planning, but a basic customer relationship management system and tools like Mention can help you track every conversation that's happening about your company. When someone mentions you, you'll be the first to know about it.

3. The Long-Term Effect of Your Coverage

Interactions and coverage help to measure short-term boosts in your campaigns, but you also need to know the long-term effectiveness of your PR efforts.

Like public relations itself, PR measurement is not static. Applying the short-term feedback you've gained to your long-term strategy is crucial for seeing the long-term impact of PR. [32] (AirPR)

When assessing the long-term effects of your coverage, consider how your brand compares to the competition with regards to readership, share of voice, media placement, and sentiment –how positive, negative, or neutral your coverage is. [33] (Cision, 2014)

These questions will help you to understand the long-term effect that your campaigns are having:
- How has my social media footprint grown in the past weeks/months/years? Have I increased my follower count, interactions, and shares?
- Have my Google rankings improved? Am I ranking better for certain keywords?
- Is my website seeing steady growth of organic traffic through referrals, search engines, and social media? [34] (Pr Daily, 2014)

A tool like Google Analytics can help to keep everything clear.

Short Versus Long-Term PR Success

Keep in mind that short-term success is usually easier to measure than the long-term impact your messaging is having. We'll give you a few examples from our own experience to illustrate our point.

Some time ago, we worked on an e-book launch with our client, UK-based contact management company Contactzilla. Our team coordinated the launch with a few well-timed media stories, increasing their email leads by 1,227% in less than two weeks. The sheer volume of awareness that we generated in such a short period of time lead to many major content partners lining up to work with our client. This is a great example of a quick win, but one that also had a lasting impact in terms of business development. It also serves as a reminder that time needs to be a consideration when assessing the value of PR.

Another exciting win is one that taught us a valuable lesson: that aspirational, opinion-based content can yield impressive results. As we saw earlier, one client-penned piece by Renters Warehouse founder Brenton Hayden generated over 82,000 page views in one day! An estimated 486,800 people saw the article on the first day that it was published (through multiple syndications) translating into roughly 16% of those readers ending up on their website. The piece received more than 4,800 comments in less than a week and generated more than 576 solid leads in under two weeks. The momentum that this piece created continued to open up opportunities for even more publicity for months to come.

Measuring long-term success may require you to go back and assess the individual achievements of your campaigns. To get a better understanding of the system we were building, we started analyzing the historical data that we had on hand for several clients.

One great example is Original Grain, a watch company that sells a line of watches that are made from whiskey barrels. We had the privilege of working closely with the founders, brothers Ryan and Andrew Beltram, on their second Kickstarter campaign.

This campaign was a tremendous success and went on to become what was at that time **one of the fastest-funded fashion Kickstarter campaigns ever**.

The success of this campaign came down to three main things:

- Riding off the long-term success of their previous Kickstarter campaign,
- Two months of intense preparation, and
- Getting samples of their watch in the hands of some pretty incredible influencers.

We knew, based on historical marketing data, that a growth-hacking and influencer-outreach approach coupled with a solid PR strategy would knock their campaign out of the park. And it did. In less than a week, we surpassed their funding goal by 436% and closed the campaign with 2,442 backers pledging USD $432,558.

In building our own process for measuring PR, we learned an important lesson: that PR has staying power. Advertising can be very much 'here today, gone tomorrow,' but a great story about your startup told in a popular media channel can live a very long and useful life.

Goal:				
Make sure your campaign supports your end goal	Monitor Interactions with your pitches	Track all brand mentions across all channels	Track all short-term and long-term coverage	Identify how your efforts contributed to your end goal
Results:				

Goal Setting For Your PR Campaign(s)

Measuring PR From Someone Who Knows

While many startups overlook the importance of measuring the success of their campaigns, tracking your successes and shortcomings is vitally important.

Christine Perkett, founder of SeeDepth PR analytics platform, advises startups to start tracking their PR metrics as soon as they begin allocating any resources towards PR activity.

If a startup is going to spend any money, or their precious time on PR, they should want to know what the return of that investment is. With the abundance of affordable tools out there for tracking metrics, and there is no reason for a startup not to begin measuring the effectiveness of their outreach immediately.

Critical to the success of PR measurement is benchmarking, something that Perkett recommends as a first step for any startup looking to measure PR. Knowing where you are now is essential to measuring your progress in the future. Startups should be keenly aware of recognizing and analyzing what's not working for them, so that they can pivot when needed without wasting precious time and resources.

For long-term success, Perkett recommends consistency in what you measure and how you measure it. This of course, will evolve with your campaigns. Choose the combination of tools to monitor, analyze, and measure, and stick with them.

Perkett highlighted a few examples of companies that do this extremely well:

SHIFT Communications. SHIFT Communications is a PR agency which has pushed forward many new ideas in PR measurement over the years. They also serve as an example to other agencies when it comes to measuring performance. According to Perkett, this company is leaps and bounds ahead of most of the agencies out there. They're also helping everyone learn through speaking, blogging, and sharing their insights.

Intralinks. Intralinks has worked to implement a global process that allows them to see how each country is contributing to their overall success. This level of analytics can be extremely challenging, but Intralinks stays consistent with their chosen tools, approach, and the data they are looking to analyze.

Jet Blue. Jet Blue is a company that thoroughly measures all of their marketing campaigns, including PR. When Perkett interviewed their EVP of Commercial and Planning, Marty St. George, he emphasized the importance of not only gathering data but also understanding what it is that you need. It always comes back to one question, he said, "What is the problem that we are trying to solve?" Jet Blue has plenty of data, but focusing on addressing the problem at hand helps them to laser-focus in on what will bring about the greatest improvement.

As you can see, measuring the success of your PR doesn't have to be difficult or complicated. Start by clarifying where your startup is now. Then set a goal, and ensure that all of your future campaigns work towards it. Next, select relevant metrics to track and look for opportunities to gather input from your team. Finally, when each campaign has finished, take the time to examine the data, feed it back through your processes, and use it to guide your long-term success.

Keep in mind that it's just as important to analyze what isn't working as it is to celebrate what has. Don't be afraid to pivot when necessary, and watch closely to see what's resonating with your audience so that you can replicate it in the future.

The To Do List:

It's time to set actionable goals for your PR strategy.

Once you've identified your objectives, you'll be able to track the success of your campaigns.

- ☐ Start by writing down a clear vision of your goals. Where is your startup now and where would you like it to be?
- ☐ Next, write down what you'll need to make it happen and break it down into actionable steps. These steps are your metrics, and you can refer to them to track your progress. Don't be afraid to involve your business partner or your team in this activity. It's important that everyone who's vested in your company's success is a part of establishing goals and metrics.
- ☐ Create a spreadsheet and use it to continually track your progress and ultimately, your results.

CHAPTER 7

THE PRESS RELEASE. WHY IT STILL EXISTS AND HOW TO USE IT

> *"When you build trust, trust follows you."*
> - COSTA VOYATZIS, EDITOR IN CHIEF, YATZER

Imagine this. Someone approaches you and asks "Hey, could you do me a favor?"

What's your reaction?

If you're like most people, chances are that your response would vary a great deal – depending on who it was asking the question.

If it's a random stranger, you'll probably be scrambling for a way to say "Sorry..." and move on. But if it's a friend, or even an acquaintance or someone who's helped you out in the past, you'd probably be quick to say "Sure...what is it?"

When it comes to PR, the situation is very much the same. You have a story that needs to be told, but it's important to ask yourself whether the recipients of it; journalists, writers, and bloggers are going to be responsive.

Do you think they would want to do you the favor of checking out your story if they've never even heard of you before?

Your best chances of getting coverage for your story depend directly upon the relationship you have with the journalist in question. For this reason, it's important for you to establish a connection and build rapport with them rather than pitching to them cold.

Building Relationships: The Human Side of PR

As important as it is, building relationships with journalists is a step that many startups and even PR reps forego. Relationships take time and a certain amount of effort, and it's much easier to just pitch at random and hope for the best. While mass pitching to strangers may occasionally work, though, this approach can actually cause more harm than good. It can drastically reduce your chances of getting coverage in the future.

Remember, journalists are people too. If you develop a reputation for spamming people with news that they aren't interested in, or stories that aren't related to their particular niche, there's a very real possibility that you'll find yourself blacklisted. And that hurts.

We believe it's worth the time and effort it takes to develop relationships because they'll pay your startup back over time. Think of building relationships with journalists like assembling your promotional team. Pitching relevant content that helps feed their cause will encourage them to cover you, and more often.

Remember our friends at Up Sonder, the drone rental company? We helped them build a relationship with Drone 360 Magazine, the drone industry's biggest drone publication. Not only did they cover Up Sonder's first big media announcement, they also covered every single one that followed. Why? Because we built and maintained our relationship with them. We didn't just ask for coverage, then go about our day. We reached out, connected, established rapport, and when they covered us, we thanked them. In fact, Up Sonder even thanked the writer by sending them a lovely bouquet of flowers. While we rarely suggest you send journalists or writers gifts, this was a special circumstance. The timing and relationship were a good fit and we know that a long-term relationship would benefit both the startup and the publication.

Managing Different Types of Coverage

Before you start, it's important to think about the type of publications that you're going to be targeting.

Remember: not all coverage is created equal. It's important to realize that there are two different types of coverage: broad, well-known publications, and niche, industry-specific publications.

Which Publications Should You Target?

- Choose your outlets based on your target customer, and your desired outcome.

- Choose broad, well-known publications: If you're looking for time in the spotlight and building brand recognition.

- Choose niche, industry-specific publications: If you're hoping to reach your target market, and generate quality leads.

Broad Coverage

Most companies would like to make it to the front page of Forbes.

And while there is value in securing big-ticket coverage and reaching a wide audience, this kind of promotion won't always produce the results that you're looking for. These publications have a huge readership, but they're also less targeted, which means that a mention alone won't set you up for life, and it won't always result in actual customers.

Targeted Coverage

This is coverage in publications that your target customer base frequents. While these publications are often much smaller, they're also much more niche – and are more likely to translate into customer conversions. This coverage is easy to overlook in favor of well-known publications, but it's important to remember that many times, smaller publications will prove to be your diamond in the rough.

In the end, securing a mix of both big-ticket and targeted coverage, and then continuing to build on the momentum that you generate is usually the best strategy.

When creating a list of publications to pitch to, ask yourself which ones your target customer reads. You can then start making a list of media that's the right fit for your startup.

Connecting With Journalists

When should you get started? Now!

Track down journalists that write for the publications you'd like coverage with, and reach out to writers, bloggers, influencers, and otherwise well-connected people that you'd like to feature your startup.

It's important to note that the days of there being one technology or business writer or editor of an outlet are very much in the past. [35] (Fast Company, 2014) Every category now branches into many subcategories, and reaching out to highly targeted niche influencers is the best way to grow brand recognition.

It's best to begin connecting with writers at least a couple of months ahead of your launch or big event. This will give you a chance to get to know the writers, and for them to learn more about you and your company.

When we started working with Original Grain, the company that we looked at in the previous chapter, we began connecting with influencers and journalists two months before the launch of their Kickstarter campaign. We commented on their posts, connected via Twitter, and kept a close eye out for ways that we could help, even if it had nothing to do with our campaign. The idea was to gain positive recognition and build rapport. When you realize that journalists see hundreds of pitches a day, the importance of standing out and being memorable becomes much clearer. Just make sure that you're doing it in a way that complements both your brand and yourself as a founder.

Building Strong Relationships

Once you've found a writer with a beat that fits your startup, you'll want to become a blip on their radar. Start by connecting with them on Twitter, LinkedIn, or Facebook; and begin to work toward creating a connection. Trust us; it's much better than pitching to them cold. If you take the time to establish yourself, interact with them, and build rapport, your chances of getting coverage will skyrocket.

When you've found a journalist or writer, consider doing the following:
- Follow their social media accounts.
- Set aside time to interact with them on social media.

- Start conversations on Twitter.
- Comment on their blog posts.
- Share their work.
- Consider sending them links to news stories that they may find interesting (Unrelated to your company, of course).
- Run a compilation story and feature one of their articles.
- Meet up with them for coffee (If they're local).
- Do this over time. Don't mass-friend them and expect media miracles to happen. This process takes weeks, if not months to do tastefully. Be patient and above all, be kind.

It's all about developing relationships and building your connections.

If you're feeling overwhelmed by the idea of making connections out of thin air – don't be. You'll experience a few rejections along the way, but that's life. Building key relationships makes it all worth it.

Keep in mind that your success with pitching will depend greatly upon the quality of the connections that you make. You'll have better luck building actual relationships with three writers than cold-pitching dozens of journalists that you don't know. Choose three or four writers, and get started.

Handling Rejection

As a startup, you're going to have to get used to hearing 'no' a lot more often than 'yes.'

Founding a startup requires passion, persistence, and eternal optimism. In the beginning, you're constantly networking, promoting, and selling the company and its long-term vision. This can lead to an over-inflated sense of accomplishment.

An ego combined with a healthy dose of rejection –being denied funding, being passed on for media coverage, or a potential client prospect saying 'no,' and it's possible that you'll spend the day with your self-esteem in the gutter. It's emotional whiplash at its finest.

Rejection doesn't feel great, but never let your ego get in the way of acknowledging that it happens to everyone. No one is spared.

The best advice is to accept the fact that rejection is a very real part of business. Don't take it personally, and most importantly, move on. Your resilience and ability to keep pressing on is essential for your survival.

Even though our team at Onboardly represented some of the fastest-growing and most exciting startups in Europe and North America, we still had to deal with rejection; a lot.

There could be any number of reasons for the rejection, including relevance, timeliness, and other external factors completely unrelated to you. Busyness is also a very real factor. People are busier than ever and time has never been a more precious commodity. By reminding yourself that it's not personal, you'll be able to make lemonade out of those inevitable lemons. If you can, try asking the journalist for advice on the best way to tackle your approach next time. If it's simply a timing issue, starting that dialogue might put things on the table for a later date.

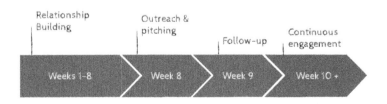

Pitching Timeline

Use Your Failures to Drive Your Future Successes

See every 'no' as an opportunity for a future 'yes.'

In the PR world, there are several categories of rejection. Each one offers a different level of insight on the ways that you can improve.

- **The 'Yes...But'**

  The kindest, gentlest form of rejection. The 'Yes...But' is the closest you can get to a 'Yes.' It either means that you've got the right pitch but wrong timing, or that your pitch needs some refinement but your idea is solid. If you receive a "Yes....But" response, work on adjusting your approach right away, scheduling a better time to discuss the idea or repositioning the pitch to get it right the second time. If you move quickly, you can still be top-of-mind and turn it into a win.

- **The 'Not Interested'**

  Use the 'Not Interested' as a way to get to know a journalist or influencer better. They've said no, but the fact they replied usually means that they respect the time that you took to reach out. Use this opportunity to reply and ask a few key questions. Look for feedback on your pitch, and ask for permission to contact them again in the future. But don't be pushy. One email follow-up to their 'Not Interested' is more than enough.

- **The 'Ignore'**

  The 'Ignore' usually goes one of two ways. It's either (a) bad timing, or (b) a bad pitch. Bad timing is often avoidable by proactively monitoring for journalists who are looking for stories. You can also subscribe to tools like HARO (Help a Reporter Out), monitor Twitter, or get to know a journalist's publication schedule. Bad pitches, on the other hand, are inexcusable. Do your homework and make sure you're targeting the right person for the topic.

- **The 'Unsubscribe'**
The ultimate learning opportunity, the 'Unsubscribe' is a classic response to a pitch gone bad. Once, in our early days, we pitched what we thought was an exciting story to a journalist. The response that we received, however, was anything but enthusiastic. It simply read: "I do not, in fact, care." Yikes. We share this flub up to merely illustrate that even the pros can mess up. The truth is —we were stretching. Upon further reflection, it's no wonder he didn't care; the topic wasn't part of his beat. Not every journalist is going to have the capacity to cover your startup, or even care for that matter.

Understanding the different forms of rejection is a measurable way to track your efforts. Work to improve your approach over time. It can be helpful to keep a log of every pitch that you send and classify the responses that you get. Your goal is to see more "Yes" and less "Unsubscribe." Keeping a log will also save you from pitching the same person twice.

When You Fail, Do It With Humility

We all make mistakes. What matters most is your ability to accept responsibility, correct them, and move forward.

A few years ago a client of ours received an unexpected letter from Getty Images, regarding an image we had inadvertently misused for a contributed post. An honest mistake, but a $1,200 one that we won't soon forget. Instead of skirting the issue or trying to sweep it under the rug, we immediately got on the phone with both Getty and the client to take full responsibility. In the end, Getty reduced the fee because we were so quick to act and we paid it without question.

You're bound to make mistakes in business and life. When you do, be swift in owning up to them.

The To Do List:

It's time to reach out! Here's how you can start building relationships with influencers and journalists in your space.

- [ ] Start creating a list of media that you'd like to have cover your startup. Include a mix of broad and targeted publications.

Now, create a plan to reach out to journalists and writers who cover the type of product or service that your company offers.

You'll want to:

- [ ] Locate relevant writers.
- [ ] Connect with them on Twitter.
- [ ] Add them to a private Twitter list.
- [ ] Start engaging with them a few times a week.
- [ ] Continue to interact with them for at least one or two months.
- [ ] Check your progress. Look back on your list and reflect on how you've grown each social relationship. Are some now following you? Have you had interesting conversations with any?
- [ ] If the timing seems right, message them asking if they mind if you send them an idea for a story.

Remember – these things take time. Don't get frustrated if you've only had a few back and forth tweets. Keep working to build rapport, and you will get there eventually.

CHAPTER 8

PERFECTING YOUR PITCH

"When we deny the story, it defines us. When we own the story, we can write a brave new ending."
- BRENE BROWN

Which would you rather own: some one-size-fits-all slippers or a handmade pair of Oxfords?

From footwear to promotional campaigns, most things are better when they're tailored. This is especially true when it comes to pitching.

The only way you'll get coverage for your story is if the journalist you target feels that it is something of interest to their readers. Reusing the same pitch is always a bad idea. You've already worked so hard to build rapport with journalists, the last thing you'd want to do is unravel everything with a cookie-cutter pitch.

Instead, it's important to take the time to master the art of the custom pitch. This is your opportunity to show the journalist exactly why your story is perfect for them.

Tailoring takes longer than mass emailing, but it's the best way to go. In the end, customizing every email is the most effective way to pitch, and the only approach that you should be taking.

Mastering the Art of the Custom Pitch

We've mentioned before that journalists are busy people. They're constantly working against deadlines and receive a tremendous amount of emails every day. In fact, roughly 44% of editors, writers, and publishers receive a minimum of twenty pitches per day! [36] (Libert, 2014)

With those odds, you're going to need more than the same old pitch to secure the coverage you're looking for.

You need a fast and effective way to show a journalist why your story will grab their reader's attention. Here are some tips for creating a memorable pitch:

1. Research the Journalist/Publication

Hopefully your initial research will have led you to someone who's a good fit for your story. If not, it's time to seek out those who would normally cover a story like yours and start building rapport.

2. Ensure Relevancy

Once you've scoped out your journalist, take the time to browse through some of their recent work and find out which type of stories they are especially interested in. Which angle do they usually take? Human interest, business, current events? You're looking for someone who covers a niche that your story fits into.

3. Find Your Hook

Go back and tweak your pitch so that it highlights the journalist's particular angle of interest. This will serve as your hook: the thing that will grab their attention and make them want to learn more.

When it comes to pitching, you have to think about the journalist or publication that you're reaching out to. Ask yourself, "Why would this matter to them?" If you're targeting a local news network, they'll be most interested in the 'local' aspect of your story. If it's an online business publication, they'll want to hear practical business advice and real-life success stories. Do your research and find an angle that will help your story stand out. It may be helpful to browse through recent headlines in publications that you're thinking of pitching, for inspiration on stories that 'sell.'

4. Keep It Concise

When you've done your research, you'll have a pretty good idea of the type of stories your desired publication or journalist is interested in. Use what you've learned to develop your pitch. Keep it short and sweet, now is not the time to tell the journalist your entire company back-story or bore them with a long-winded press release. Remember that your end goal is to interest a journalist enough to make them want to learn more. Be interesting and relevant. This is your opportunity to stand out from the crowd, don't take it lightly.

5. Be the Odd Man Out

Journalists get so many pitches every day, it's going to take something unusual, and often downright shocking, to beat the others to the prize.

What does it take to grab their attention? A pitch that's interesting and enticing. Be bold, be daring, and yes, even be a little weird. Especially if it's consistent with your brand.

At Onboardly, we were always proud to be a little different. We had strong imaginations and lots of exciting ideas. We weren't afraid to share our love of dorky things. Every company has fun or interesting quirks that make them unique. We always encouraged our clients to embrace them. They'll make your pitch, and your story, different. Channel that inner weirdness and use it to set your startup apart.

6. Stop Trying to Pretend That You're Normal

Let's be frank. Normal people rarely make history. Normal doesn't get remembered, and the same is true with brands. To make a lasting impression, you must break away from the norm and dare to be different.

Do you have an opinion that you know will ruffle some feathers? Great. Doing things differently? Perfect. These are the types of stories journalists want! No one is interested in your quarterly reports, or hearing about how your company is doing the same thing that a different startup did last year.

7. Be Weird Yet Approachable

Don't be that cool kid from high school that everyone was afraid to talk to. The last thing you'd want is for your company to come off as standoffish. Be accessible; a brand that customers can identify with. Make people laugh and give journalists something they want to publish.

8. Own Your Brand

Even if you follow the tips we've outlined, if you don't truly own your brand, you'll come off as inauthentic.

Believe us when we say that people can quickly tell when your alignment is off. Do yourself a favor and evaluate the image your company is presenting. Are you compelling? Funny? Interesting? Attractive? Or are you just another face in the crowd? Own your personality and your brand, and embrace what makes you unique. Confidence goes a long way but so does approachability. Your startup's 'weird' traits will make it real and memorable to your customers. As a bonus, these traits give the media something memorable to latch onto, helping that pitch of yours to stand out.

If your pitches just aren't landing, it may be time to go back to the drawing board and figure out what truly makes your startup different. Don't send another pitch until you do.
But if you follow the above steps, and nothing makes a difference, there's a chance that you may have an 'ugly baby' on your hands

So You Think You Have an Ugly Baby. How Can You Tell?

In many ways, ideas are like babies. Everyone thinks theirs is the best. As founders, we're all guilty of thinking that our 'baby' is Gap Kids ad-worthy, when in reality a journalist wouldn't feel that our product is even remotely newsworthy. You might believe that your concept is fascinating, but if you have a challenging or extremely niche product, then you may be the only one.

In our experience, an idea that's hard to sell is usually due to one of the following reasons.

1. Your Product Is Subpar

It could be something as simple as not having your technical ducks in a row, or it could be that your product just isn't that good. It's hard to stomach, but it happens more often than you might think.

2. You're in a 'Boring' Industry

If this is true for your startup, you're in good company. Many businesses are solving a real problem, but lack that inherent 'wow' factor.

3. Your Positioning Is Weak

Your product or service addresses a gap in the market and solves a real problem, but you don't have a compelling story that speaks directly to your target customer. There's also a good chance that you don't have a refined strategy to grab the media's attention.

If you fall into the first category, we have bad news. No amount of marketing or PR can solve the customer dissatisfaction that a poor product causes.

But if you find your startup in categories #2 or #3, there's hope for you yet. People find your industry boring because your brand positioning is weak; these two problems are interconnected. The truth is, you cannot rely on the merits of your product to win over your audience. You have to do the PR legwork to get people on board.

So let's get started.

How to Pitch an Ugly Baby

It's relatively common for startups to develop a product or service that just doesn't sound as cool to everyone else as it does to them. If it's happened to you, don't worry, we've got some ways to help you close the perception gap between you and your audience:

1. Know Yourself

It sounds simple enough, but many startups don't take the time to have a real heart-to-heart with themselves. In developing your startup story, you've already got a leg up on the competition, but it doesn't hurt to have a bit of a refresher before you start planning your pitch. Ask yourself these critical questions:

- Who is your startup?
- What is your product or service?

- What problem does it solve?
- Who needs this problem resolved?
- What is the best way to reach these people?

Think about this like putting yourself back through Marketing 101: you have to nail down your brand positioning, target audience, and outreach method before you even dream of pressing send on that email to a journalist. And don't feel that your product is too complicated or niche to explain clearly. Being unable to explain the product in a clear, succinct way most likely indicates that you need to go back to the drawing board, and uncover the true essence of your startup.

2. Let Your Inner Hemingway Out

It's time to unleash your inner Hemingway! Get into the mind of your favorite author and articulate why you like their particular style. Then borrow their tactics, adapting them to your own storytelling needs.

3. Give Them Something They Want to Read

Your true audience will never pass up intriguing, relevant, and well-delivered content. Start thinking about how to integrate content into your PR strategy as a way to show people your industry, and your product or service.

4. Get Honest Feedback

There's something therapeutic about getting real, brutally honest feedback. It helps us move forward and progress rather than remaining unaware and complacent.

Here are some ways to get honest feedback on your pitch and

product:

- Get the opinions of the handful of people. You know who they are, they're the ones with a track record of being brutally honest with you.
- Get anonymous feedback from your employees.
- Survey early beta testers.

Continually working on your brand positioning and seeking out feedback will help you nail down the most interesting aspects of your product.

Getting Your Ugly Baby Media Ready

To quote a common adage, beauty is in the eye of the beholder. And right now, you're probably the only beholder! It's time for you to figure out a way to share the love you have for your product with the right journalists; ones who will see its value the way you do.

If you're struggling to gain traction, try the following:

1. Build Relationships in Advance

Hopefully you've already taken our advice when it comes to this, but in case you haven't, start building relationships in advance. If you don't, you will likely remain unknown in the endless sea of startups.

2. Develop Your Filter

Not everything is pitchable. The sooner you realize that no one cares unless you give them a reason to, the better. Knowing your target journalists is an integral part of building relationships in advance. If you know what they're interested in, you'll be able to tell a story that they'll care about.

Here are some questions to ask yourself if you still need some help identifying them:

- What do they write about?
- Have they written about my competitor's product?
- Have they written about a problem that my product or service solves?
- Do they have an interest outside of their 'standard' that I can appeal to?

3. Target Journalists Who Will Say Yes

This may seem obvious, but if you're a small fish in a big pond, you're not going to get anywhere chasing the big guys. Unless, of course, you have a proven track record of successful product launches. If you're new to the startup scene, your success rate will be much higher if you go after the 'small fish.' There are plenty of talented junior journalists who aren't at the constant mercy of pitches and as a result are easier to reach. Often, they are just as talented as the big ones, but have just entered the game so may have more time to give to you. And if they cover your niche outlet, they're probably the most qualified person to write about you anyway.

4. Choose Realistic Outlets

You'll gain better traction when your goals are realistic. If you wouldn't publish your own story in Venture Beat or The Next Web, then your startup probably isn't at a mature enough stage to be covered by major publications. Instead of going straight to TechCrunch, consider targeting the smaller publications first. They'll be the most excited about your product, and will help you establish the building blocks necessary to get you in those big publications.

5. Develop a Newsworthy Hook

Newsworthiness will depend upon your industry as well as the outlet and journalist that you are reaching out to. Do your research and figure out what's going on in the news. Consider the most relevant and surprising ways that you can add to that discussion. Spend time crafting headlines and story variations. Your goal is to create an irresistible story that's impossible to turn down.

6. Make the Media Come to You

When you're not pitching to journalists, think about the ways you can bring the news to you. Pull a stunt, give back, run a contest, join industry events, or if you're feeling especially brave, dare to disagree with someone; as long as it's not a stance that will negatively impact your brand. These are all great opportunities for you to score earned media, even if you're not a bright or flashy company.

A Word of Caution: Five Startup PR Mistakes to Avoid

Pitching can be a challenge without the right tools, efforts, and contacts and if you're going it alone you probably don't have the connections most startup publicists have. To help you in your journey, and to save you from making some of the classic mistakes that startups and even some PR pros make, here are a few key mistakes to avoid.

Mistake #1: Mass Pitching

Picture this, your launch day is approaching and you've done no groundwork in terms of media outreach. You have a list of tech journalists from a friend, and figure it won't hurt to send out a mass email to them all.

STOP. Take a second and think about what you're doing. First, have you stopped to consider who these writers are and what they write about? Remember that the term 'tech journalist' is a broad one in today's world. If your startup has built an Android app, you're not likely going to get too far with a Mac-loving iPhone-using tech writer.

Remember the whiskey barrel watch guys at Original Grain? They hired us three months before their planned launch. During that time, we mapped out detailed and personalized lists of journalists and publications that we knew would love these watches. We started pitching about two months before the launch even happened, because we knew we'd get a few "I'm too busy," or "I'm on leave" responses. We even allowed for 6-8 weeks to send sample watches to journalists once we connected with them, accounting for things like shipping delays and a journalist's busy schedule. We wanted to make sure they had plenty of time to try the watch out for themselves. You may think that starting two months in advance of a launch seems ridiculous, but it helped to buy us just the right amount of time to land features in TechCrunch, Gizmodo, The Awesomer, and more. The wait was definitely worth it.

Instead of mass pitching, always do your research.

Let's say you've invented an app that will revolutionize the way people travel and book flights, accommodations, and tours. Instead of blindly pitching any writer at the outlet you're interested in, take a moment to search travel apps on their website. Have your competitors been covered in the past? Is there one particular writer who tends to cover travel stories and apps?

Learning who's done what will help you hone in on the right writer to cover your story. There is no guarantee that they will cover you, but if you're pitching to the best writer for the job, you increase your odds greatly.

The Biggest Blunder: *Contacting a poor fit for your story*

Don't assume that you know a writer or journalist if you haven't been following their work for a while. Not only will this upset them, it's almost guaranteed that your email will look desperate, and will quickly end up in their trash folder.

Mistake #2: Emailing Their Work and Personal Address

You've identified your writer and have found their work email, but also stumbled upon their Gmail address while taking a look at their personal social media accounts. If you're thinking "I can get to them quicker if I use their personal accounts" you're wrong! Unless they have given you permission to reach out to them there, then you are just digging yourself a bigger hole.

What do you do?

When you have two separate emails for a writer, it is a professional courtesy to ping them at their work email. Personal emails are just that, personal. While it may get to them more efficiently, it's not the email they normally conduct business with. By reaching out to them at their work email, you earn points for following the rules.

But what if you can only find their personal email?

Some situations will arise where a writer's work email is untraceable. But thanks to the power of Google, you've managed to find a personal email via their Tumblr, personal blog or Facebook account. This begs the question: Is it appropriate to email their personal account?

In these cases, unless a writer has specifically expressed that their personal email is not for submitting story pitches, proceed. Most writers who publicly offer their personal email via personal sites will specifically mention that it is for personal inquiries only, and not inquiries related to their job.

The Biggest Blunder: *Emailing both their personal and work emails.*

Just don't do it! The response is never pretty.

Mistake #3: Failing to Personalize

Mass pitching is bad, but sending impersonal pitches is up there too. It's easy to draft a pitch and simply hit copy and paste, but you should avoid doing so at all costs.

If you know the writer's name, use it! If you know a particular story they have covered recently, or one that is relevant or led you to them, mention it. Include the name of the publication or media outlet in your email. Add any personal touches you can to allude to the idea that they are the only one you are pitching to, and that they are special.

For example, I've often taken things from a journalist's Twitter profile to incorporate into my pitch. Once, I was pitching a Huffington Post writer, and I noticed that her bio mentioned her love of sloths. Since I love sloths as well, I ended my pitch with my favorite sloth GIF. Personalized touches can sometimes make all the difference.

Using sentences such as, "I wanted to make sure you got this first," or "I wanted to personally send this to you myself" can also help to personalize the email, and will make the writer feel respected and important.

The Biggest Blunder: *Pretending to be their new best friend.*

While it is good to add a personal touch or two to show authenticity, there is a line that can easily be crossed. Just because you've gone over their Twitter bio and scrolled through their personal blog doesn't mean you should act as though you know them. Always treat them professionally.

Mistake #4: Cold Pitching on Twitter

A cold pitch tweet is just as bad as a cold pitch email or phone call. If you've never interacted with this writer before, now is not the time to tweet them with a request to cover your startup. Give yourself some extra time to properly initiate contact with the writer.

Instead, create a private list of writers that you're interested in pitching, and actively monitor them. When a subject matter you can relate to comes up, tweet a reply or comment. Engage with them at least three to five times before pitching them. When you feel confident, start by sending them a quick tweet, like: "Hey - I'm working on something that might interest you, any chance I can ping you?" If they respond and express interest, follow with, "Excellent. What's the best way to reach you?" This opens the door for them to provide you with their email or indicate that you can continue via direct message.

If they decline, don't flush your hard work down the drain. Offer a response like, "I understand. Thanks for the reply!" instead. While the timing or story content may not be right for them now, you may have something for them in the future, so always be respectful and continue to engage long after the pitch has been made.

Also, keep in mind that your Twitter history will also come back to either serve or haunt you. If you're using your personal Twitter account to make these pitches, which is usually the best option, make sure that you have consistently been respectful, and active. A writer will look you up and if they don't like what they see they will ignore you or even block you.

And above all, if you're sending out additional tweets to journalists to pitch them, make sure you're spreading out these tweets with other non-pitch related content. No journalist wants to go to your Twitter feed and see you've pitched five other journalists in the last 20 minutes. That won't end well.

The Biggest Blunder: *Failing to use Twitter etiquette.*

Twitter's 280 character limit appeals to busy writers or journalists, so keep your pitch brief and concise. If they're interested, they'll offer you an alternate means of contact to speak further.

Mistake #5: Disappearing Immediately After a Pitch

If you pitch a writer and they respond, don't fall off the grid. Your schedule is busy and things come up, but if you really want the story, be sure to provide them with a reply within 24 hours, even if it's just to say that you will get back to them as soon as you can.

An 'out of office' message should not be a replacement for your response. Again, if you're after story coverage, you must put in the effort to receive it. All media materials, such as media advisories and media kits, should be ready to go before you begin pitching for this same reason. You need to be prepared when a writer expresses interest.

The Biggest Blunder: *Not responding at all.*

Maybe you've found an alternate writer or media publication that suits your startup better. Maybe you've decided to halt the launch and stay in private beta longer. Either way, never leave a writer hanging. If the circumstances have changed, offer up an explanation, or if necessary, an apology promptly. Remember that you may want to work with this writer again, so be respectful.

By keeping these things in mind, you'll be able to make your pitching life a little bit easier, and more effective as well.

What to Expect When You're Pitching

You're going to experience both wins and rejection in the world of pitching. To help the process go a lot more smoothly, and to give you an indication that you're on the right track, here are a few things that you can expect when you're pitching.

- You will experience rejection. You will be ignored. You will be told your startup/story isn't interesting.
- Use each rejection as a learning opportunity. Go back and see where you failed to personalize, or where you made a mistake in choosing which journalist to pitch your story to. You will need to tweak your pitch every time you learn a valuable lesson.
- Start small. Don't dismiss smaller outlets or lesser-known journalists; they can help you to secure relevant traffic and establish credibility on your way to those bigger publications.
- Remember that just because a journalist covered your technology or industry once, doesn't mean that they are the one to pitch. It's best to pitch journalists who have covered your industry or topic on more than two or three isolated occasions.
- You and your team will need to know your product or service offering inside and out.
- You will need to expect hard-hitting questions from journalists. Be prepared and know your facts so that you're capable of making every opportunity count for your startup. You should also sure you know how to handle questions that you may not be willing to discuss like funding, investors, bad reviews, or criticisms of your company.
- You will often be working against deadlines.
- Some of your best opportunities will come out of nowhere.

- If your pitch lands with a particular journalist, great! Make sure that you keep that rapport going, but keep in mind that news coverage needs to be ongoing to be effective. Don't stop researching and developing relationships with other journalists simply because you've found one to work with right now.

Finally, above all, a little bit of common sense will come in handy when it comes to crafting and sending out your pitches. Asking yourself "Would I respond to this?" can save you from wasting your time sending out a contrived, impersonal, or unorganized pitch. Knowing at least a little bit about the person that you're sending the pitch to, will help you to craft it in a way that will elicit the best response.

Prepare yourself and your team; rejection is bound to happen and it will come in many forms, especially when you're just starting out. But you don't have to start over at square one every time you experience a setback. Instead, learn from the experience and build on it, using it to improve your strategy. As you do, you'll begin to hear 'Yes' a lot more often.

The To Do List:

It's time to write your pitch!

- ☐ Find a journalist who's a good fit
- ☐ Keep it concise
- ☐ Be the odd man out
- ☐ Stop trying to pretend that you're normal
- ☐ Be weird yet approachable (If it fits your brand)
- ☐ Own your brand

Concerned you may have an ugly baby?
Let's find out:

- ☐ Start pitching your product to family, friends, and strangers.
- ☐ Ask friends or colleagues to introduce you to mutual friends who will be unbiased and are open to hearing your pitch.
- ☐ Gather as much feedback as possible and encourage people to be honest.

Most importantly, have fun with this activity. You can learn about your product when you start pitching it to others.

CHAPTER 9

BE PREPARED: ARE YOU READY FOR WHEN THE MEDIA COMES KNOCKING?

"Dig deep. Tell your story."
- MARK SCHAEFER

You've mastered the art of pitching and are waiting for the media to come knocking. Now, let's make sure you're ready for when they do.

When you invest time and money in the right PR strategy, the payoff can be tremendous. It can lead to increased brand exposure, early product traction, and interested investors. As Bill Gates himself said, "If I was down to my last dollar, I'd spend it on PR." While not every startup can, or should invest in PR, there are some definite signs that indicate that your startup is ready to take on the challenge.

Let's focus on the two that will be most important for you at this stage in the game: knowing what your product does, and appointing your company spokesperson.

1. You Know What Your Product Does: And Can Articulate It

No matter how complicated your product or service is, at this point, you have to be able to distill its purpose down to a few short sentences. You've already considered your story, and figured out what makes your team and product special. It should be relatively simple now to clearly and succinctly express the problem that your product solves. Go ahead and reread your startup story, even if it's just a rough draft, to figure out what the true essence of your company is. It's likely that you set out to solve a problem, either one you had yourself, or one that you saw in your particular market. You then designed your product or service to address that problem. Your startup story explains all of this in detail, but to be truly media ready, you need to be able to capture the essence of what your company/product does in two or three sentences; your elevator pitch, if you will.

Simplify your product description

If you're still wondering why this distillation matters, here's a quick example.

Consider Le Tote, a fashion-for-hire startup. Le Tote's slogan, Always Have Something New To Wear, is simple and succinct. What woman wouldn't want access to new apparel every month for only $59? Said to be the "Netflix for clothing," Le Tote has been able to establish itself, raise money, and expand its product base not because it's disrupting the fashion industry, but because it stuck to its core offering. With clear and polished messaging, it now stands as a highly recognized brand.

We recently interviewed Le Tote's CEO Rakesh Tondon about his experience with PR; something that he used to spread the word about what his company was doing. Tondon stressed that PR proved to be an especially powerful way to talk about Le Tote and how it worked; specifically when it came to highlighting the need for their service. If the message they were sending out about hadn't been as laser-focused, it's possible that Le Tote would not have experienced the success they've had today.

Being able to walk into any situation and tell others exactly what you do, and why you do it is incredibly powerful. Never underestimate the impact that clear messaging can have on your company.

2. You've Appointed a Company Spokesperson

Another step to media readiness is having a 'face' or spokesperson for your startup. When it comes down to it, the best spokesperson is almost always your founder. After all, who else could better explain exactly what your company does, and why, than the person who created it?

If you're the founder of the company, it's time for you to step up to the plate. You have a wealth of knowledge, a long-term vision, and a personal investment in the success of your company, and it's nearly impossible to replicate your authenticity and passion.

When you think of awesome startups, their founder often comes to mind: Steve Jobs of Apple, Drew Houston of Dropbox, Marc Nager of Startup Weekend. Being the founder is part of your story, so use it to your advantage.

3. Your Spokesperson Is Ready for the Media

If you're feeling uneasy about your role as the spokesperson, consider some coaching. A PR firm can teach you the best way to communicate your story to the public. They will introduce you to a valuable professional network, and can identify useful events or speaking opportunities that will help you to build your reputation. You could also have a look at our guide, 'How to be Ready for the Spotlight: The Founder's Guide to Looking Ridiculously Good Online' for more advice on getting media ready. [37] (Warren, 2016)

You're going to need a particular set of skills in order to come across as media ready.

Refine Your Skills:

- **Be the Speaker of the House**: Solid speaking skills are an absolute must as a startup founder. Improve your skills with practice, by researching your audience, and by learning to how tell compelling stories.

- **Prepare Yourself for Questioning**: Consider holding some mock media interviews with people on your team. Have them ask you both the easy and the hard questions. Learn to turn your potential weaknesses into strengths and practice humility.

- **Don't Lose Yourself:** You're not a robot, but many founders come across this way, especially online. Don't be guilty of memorizing the story and forgetting your own unique personality in the process. It can come through in many different ways, so don't forget to let it out sometimes.

- **Be Consistent:** Don't risk losing credibility by being inconsistent in the way you show up and the stories that you tell. Everything changes, but the core principles you build in being media-ready won't. Eventually, consistency won't even be a challenge if you're doing it right.

Next, there are some practical steps that you can take to get ready for the media.

Practical Steps:

- **Start With Google**: Ahh, everyone's old pal Google. The first tool we all usually use to get to know someone we don't know yet. Take this opportunity to search for yourself, and see what others will find when they type your name in. Do a search for your name, and one for your company name + your name. Good, bad, or ugly; it could probably be better. Take this time to clean up and polish your online presence. Get rid of old profiles, and delete your high school Tumblr account.

- **Get Some New Photos:** Consider what photos you will provide when asked for a headshot, and the photo that you'll use on your social media accounts. Do yourself a favor and get some professional pictures taken. Cropping your high school graduation photo just isn't going to cut it anymore.

- **Stick to the Script**: Or at least be aware of it. Being absolutely clear on your mission and your talking points will give you a leg up for moments when improvisation is a necessity. Consistency is important, so be sure that the story that you're telling is the same one everyone at your startup is.

When you've taken the time to get yourself ready for the limelight, spruced up your image, and have your key messaging down, it's time to take a look at one final step: preparing your media kit.

4. You've Put Together Your Media Kit

Many founders find themselves wondering whether they should have a media kit at all. But for startups and growing companies, having a kit full of details is incredibly important.

Put simply; your media kit is a collection of materials about your company that makes it easy for a journalist to tell your story. It provides the media with a compelling glimpse into your startup, inviting them to reach out to you for more information. A media kit is an often-essential component for gaining media coverage, and can be an extremely useful way to convey information.

Your kit needs to be exciting, enticing, and easy to access. Most importantly, it needs to be the place journalists can go to get the information that they need.

Your Media Kit Should Include:

- **Your Press Release or Video Pitch:** Your press release is your chance to shine. It is a high-level summary of your company story and your product or service offering. It should include a positioning statement, and highlight the important features of your product. In should also include the major points that the press need to know about your launch, including information on your company and its founders. This is your opportunity to clearly articulate the problem that your startup is tackling, and give strong arguments for the solution you're providing. Although it should be filled with key information, you'll want to avoid writing a monologue packed with tedious details. Instead, use it to show the world how amazing your product, service, or company is!

- **Three to Four Versions of Your Story:** Not every publication will be interested in the same version of your story. Feel free to highlight aspects of your story that you feel will be most compelling to the journalist/publication that you're pitching to. As always, it all comes down to making sure you've done your research so that you can customize your story and make it truly irresistible!

- **Logo(s) and Screenshots:** Include your company logo(s) as well as screenshots of your product or service in action. Don't forget to include several orientations for multiple site formats/backgrounds. Having great images will help readers to better relate to your product or service. Journalists want images to complement their stories, so you make their job easier by providing them up front.

- **Founders Bios:** While a journalist will rarely publish them as is, a bio can give context to a well-rounded story. Sometimes a founder story can be even more compelling than your product, and can have an equal impact on a reader's interest in your startup.

A quick but powerful example comes from the story of 15Five founder David Hassell, who we looked at earlier on. His founder story begins by telling the reader of his deep desire to help people reach their fullest potential at work. It goes on to mention his method of soliciting ideas and feedback from employees and colleagues, and explains how that led to the creation of their product. His story gives context to the beginnings of 15Five, and shows how his vision led to a product that's now helping over 1,000 successful companies. [38] (15Five)

- **A Selection of Great Photos:** Include high-quality photos or videos of your product or service in action. Team photos are also a hit with journalists, so be sure to include those as well. Company headshots add personality to your story and screenshots can inspire your readers to become customers. As this is your ultimate goal, be sure your photos are as compelling as possible.

- **Sell Sheet or Fact Sheet:** Sales sheets and information on market opportunities and the potential of your product or service can help a journalist to tell your story. They can offer unique story angles for the press to pursue that are different from the usual stories they cover. Odds are that you've prepared a fact sheet for investors or pitches that contain information about the market opportunity (potential) and where your product or service fits into the ecosystem. If you have a fact sheet that positions your startup favorably and has strong facts and statistics to support that positioning, include it

- **Proof of Concept (Statistics):** Journalists are always on the lookout for human interest stories. If you have any interesting case studies or customer success stories, be sure to include them. Providing real-life testimonies with links to studies that back up your concept is also a good idea.

- **Your Contact Information**: As the purpose of your kit is to make journalists want to know more, be sure to provide them with a few different ways to reach you so that they can get additional information.

Make sure that you keep things up-to-date. Nothing is worse than an outdated kit full of unorganized materials. Your media kit is not a catch-all for random tidbits about your company. It is there to pique journalists' interest and help them tell your story. Don't give them a random pile of things to sift through, or they may end up moving on to a story that's easier to cover.

As your company grows, you'll be able to add more to your media kit. News stories, feature articles, major milestones, and anything that can help the press to tell your story are great additions. Continually update it with new data, press releases, or other supporting evidence, and make sure that your links are valid.

A media kit isn't supposed to be created and then left to gather dust. It's a work in progress that needs to evolve as your startup does. At first, you might feel as though your kit is a bit sparse, but as you begin to secure coverage, you will soon have more to add to it.

A Friendly Reminder...

Your story should always take center stage. No amount of facts, sales sheets, and bios can save you if you don't have a compelling narrative.

The most memorable startups are those with a great story to tell. If you find yourself pressed for time, you should focus on your story, rather than perfecting the finer points of your media kit. Although important, these aren't as vital as your story. Some journalists won't ask for a media kit at all, or if they do, they may ask you for something specific, like an interview, a link to product shots, or a press release. If they do ask you for company information and you don't have a media kit ready to send off, you could always direct them to your website's 'about us' page or send them some high-level bullet points.

Communicating successfully requires compelling content. If you aren't interesting, you can be certain that you won't gain much traction outside of your own four walls. The more intriguing you are, or can make yourself out to be, the more likely journalists will be to take notice.

When you build your media kit properly, what looks like a simple little package of goods can become your ultimate secret weapon to securing great coverage. Consider using a personalized Dropbox folder or Google Drive for each journalist that you approach, so that you can easily share by inviting them to the folder. Both of these programs will confirm when they join or view the folder, confirming that they at least have some interest in your story.

A Media Kit Case Study: Rent Frock Repeat

A fantastic example of a media kit that we worked on at Onboardly comes from Rent frock Repeat (like Rent the Runway in the USA), a wardrobe solution for women across Canada. With Rent frock Repeat, customers can sign up for a free membership to their service online, find a dress that they love, rent it, and then return it.

Their media kit includes beautiful pictures of some of the dresses available for rent and then goes on to outline their market as, Women 28-55 years old (average age 34.4). Less concerned with labels and more concerned about looking appropriate and feeling great while doing so. The company also provides a clear avatar of their customer, with details such as:
- She dislikes shopping or is over-scheduled and wants a one-stop shop that will provide her with everything she needs for

her event.
- She doesn't always understand fashion and is not necessarily interested in it.
- She wants to take the thinking, time, and anxiety out of what she is going to wear.

Their kit then shows the simple, two-step process this customer would go through in order to use their service, provides a great photo of the founders, and follows with a Media Q&A that is a fun and innovative way of providing details about their company.

From the kit, the journalist can easily see the inspiration behind the company. They can read about how the founders didn't want to spend money on yet another dress that would only be worn once to a wedding. They designed Rent frock Repeat to solve a problem they had themselves. This part of their media kit also gives journalists a look at their process; that is, how they go about selecting the best dress styles for their members.

The kit ends with their contact information, indicating where a journalist can ask questions or request more images or interviews with the founders. It also includes their webpage as well as Facebook and Twitter handles. [39] (Onboardly)

Using Your Media Kit Effectively

Aside from sending out your media kit to journalists and waiting for them to respond, you also extend its impact by placing it in a 'newsroom' on your company website.

Here are two great examples of companies that have done this:

- Uber

  Uber has a page on their website that is dedicated to their news, and the information for their media kit. [40] (Uber) It's a place where they post relevant blog posts from members of their team and provide a spot for journalists to download approved logos, photography, and app scenes from around the world. They also have a section that allows journalists to contact them for further details.

- **Trulia**

    Another great example of an online newsroom comes from Trulia, an online real estate site for home buyers, sellers, and renters. [41] (Trulia) Their 'media room' contains different pages for their most recent press release, company information, news stories, blogs, and research. Like Uber, they have a section for downloading their most up-to-date product screenshots, b-roll footage, logos, and executive headshots. They also have their contact information for journalists with additional questions, making it interesting by assuring anyone who is interested in contacting them that they are, "Helpful, smart and good looking."

These are large companies that likely have many journalists wanting to cover them at any given moment, but just because you're not Uber doesn't mean there isn't a journalist out there just itching to cover a story like yours. And there's no reason why you can't put their strategies to work for you.

It's important to realize that success leaves clues. Take a look at some well-known or newsworthy companies, and see what they're doing for PR. Then, consider how you can make those same ideas work for you on a smaller scale.

Are You Up for the Challenge?

Ultimately, all great PR comes from a willingness to put in the work. It takes time, and effort, but your secret to securing coverage involves having an excellent narrative that's irresistible to the journalist, and making it as easy as possible for them to tell that story, thanks to your media kit. It also means being ready for the press –knowing exactly what your product does, and being able to articulate it professionally. Finally, it means brushing up your public speaking skills –and knowing how to answer the easy questions, and what to say when the difficult ones roll in.

The To Do List:

Getting ready for the press can seem overwhelming, but it doesn't have to be. Here's a checklist that outlines the steps that you should take to make sure you're all set.

Ensure Media Readiness:

- ☐ Clean up your online presence.
- ☐ Get some new photos.
- ☐ Stick to the script.
- ☐ Polish your speaking skills and learn to tell compelling stories.
- ☐ Prepare yourself for challenging questions.
- ☐ Don't be a robot. Find a way to inject personality into your interviews and stories.
- ☐ Be consistent with your messaging.

Building a media kit should be a fun time for you and your team. Make a list of everything you would like to include. Be creative, and don't be afraid to think big. When you start creating your kit, come back to these notes and check each item off when it's complete.

Here are some important items that you'll want to think about including in your media kit:

Your Media Kit:

- ☐ Your Press Release or Video Pitch
- ☐ Three to Four Versions of Your Story
- ☐ Logo(s) and Screenshots

- [ ] Founders Bios
- [ ] A Selection of Great Photos
- [ ] Sell Sheet or Fact Sheet
- [ ] Proof of Concept (Statistics)
- [ ] Your Contact Information

CHAPTER 10

GAINING TRACTION WHEN THE MEDIA WON'T COVER YOU

"Don't judge each day by the harvest you reap, but by the seeds you plant."
- ROBERT LOUIS STEVENSON

What your company is doing is amazing. You're breaking new ground, forging new paths, and taking the road less traveled.

There's just one problem: no one knows it but you.

The thing is, you need media attention. You need your story heralded from the rooftops, and given credibility by credible folk. But TechCrunch and Forbes aren't exactly knocking at your door. You've spent months preparing a product for launch and then, crickets. The media is simply not interested. What went wrong? What do you do?

Many are quick to blame their marketing efforts or their PR

team. While this certainly could be the case, often the reason most media won't cover a story is because of bad timing, a bad product, or too many competitors in the market all launching at the same time. It could also be that the journalist is simply overworked, and has no time. Even the best pitch or story can be ignored, and sometimes it's due to reasons that are beyond your control.

Still, there are some simple things that you can do to increase your chance of media coverage.

1. Know Who You Are

This might not sound glamorous, but it's important. Make sure you know who you are, and have your company messaging down pat. And present yourself in a way that will connect with your audience. It's important to present a real and genuinely likable image. If your audience can't connect with you, you won't win them over. Go over your key messaging again. What makes your company unique? How are you different from the competition? How are you better? Be prepared to answer those questions well and concisely. If you don't have that knowledge, then as far as your audience is concerned, you don't have anything worth sharing. [42] (First Round Review, n.d.)

2. Join Communities and Forums

If you aren't already actively on Reddit, Quora, Product Hunt, HackerNews, Inbound.org, and other relevant industry sites, it's time to start participating. Many of these established communities rank well in search, have a large and active participant base, and people willing to help you either promote your company or answer your burning questions. It's important to schedule time every day to use these resources. The more you contribute and participate, the more you will get out of them. If you don't have the time, then give access to your marketing team or a dedicated online guru who can ramp things up for you. The key is to start actively using these communities months before you really 'need' them. And hey, who knows what you can learn there anyway.

3. Start Newsjacking

Look for opportunities to take what's happening in the world, and make it work for you. Take a look at trends or current events and find a way to relevantly tie them to what your startup is doing. The trick is to do this like a pro. Anyone can newsjack, but to be successful you have to have a keen eye and be timely. Author and speaker David Meerman Scott says that newsjacking is, "The art of injecting your ideas into a breaking news story, so that you can become a part of the story." [43] (Scott) Take a look at what's happening out there in the world, and find a way to make it work for your startup.

A fantastic example of newsjacking comes from former President Obama's 2011 visit to Darwin Australia. Chief Minister of the Northern Territory, Paul Henderson and the Territory Insurance Office said that they planned to gift the President a $50,000 insurance policy against crocodile attacks upon his landing. Of course, it was well-known that the CIA and the President's security team weren't going to let him anywhere near crocodiles that could attack, but the insurance company made the fact that he was coming to their territory work for them. Not only that, but they played into the fact that the policy would help to give Michelle Obama and his daughters "peace of mind" while he visited, and also that it would be a gift unlike any he's ever received. Talk about making a Presidential visit a part of your narrative! [44] (ABC News, 2011)

4. Create Commenting Lists

Consider creating lists of blogs and company or influencer Facebook pages to like, subscribe to, and comment on. Business Facebook pages have a woeful lack of engagement and taking the time to engage with others on social media or blogs is a great way to get noticed. When it comes to blog comments, just remember to be smart and helpful with your comments. Your intention should be to provide substance that will help to start a conversation.

5. Publish on Other Platforms

Want attention that you can count on each month? Why not consider a Medium account for your startup where your founder or team members aim to publish at least one post a month about company milestones, exciting news, or new product features. Some companies choose to do this in addition to press releases; others scratch the press release altogether and rely on Medium to share their company successes.

6. Complete an Audit

We all hate the word 'audit,' but in this case, it's totally worth your time. Check back on the marketing initiatives that have completely failed and nip them in the bud. After one or two months you should have a clear understanding of what works and what doesn't. Focus your limited marketing dollars on the channels that are converting. Don't be lured into feeling that you have to keep up with every social media channel. If your target audience isn't hanging out there, then walk the other way.

I recently overheard a well-known startup marketer say, "I am still trying to figure out Snapchat." The fact is that most people won't "get" every single social media channel. Pay close attention to where your customers are already hanging out online and go there. You don't have to be everywhere.

7. Secure Some Speaking Gigs

Polish your public speaking skills and get rid of those nerves. If you want to really stand out, it's time you take the stage. With the myriad of events these days, there is surely something in your city that relates to your industry. Become a member of local entrepreneur Facebook groups, your local Chamber of Commerce, and other associations that allow for guest speaking opportunities. Create a professional speaking profile, such as a separate landing page on your website, with links to your social accounts and videos of you speaking. Michael Hyatt, well-known author, speaker, and leading virtual mentor does this incredibly well. [45] (Michael Hyatt) If you haven't been videotaped before, let alone stood up on stage, start by creating a mini-series of two-minute videos explaining some industry hacks. It's a sure-fire way to increase your presence and create your official speaking portfolio.

Once you've completed this page, put yourself out there and start reaching out to event organizers offering a free talk for their event. If you've done your homework, created a professional portfolio, and contacted the right person, you'll start getting speaking gigs before you know it. Keep at it and you'll be an expert in no time.

While the list of potential PR tactics is endless, these seven are sure to help kickstart your game, allowing you to gain valuable media attention when all else has failed.

The To Do List:

If the media is still not knocking at your door, what do you do?

Whether you're having a hard time securing media coverage or have had great coverage but are wondering what to do next, write down one or two items from the above suggestions that interest you.

- [ ] Jot down the high-level steps you will need to take next to make them happen.
- [ ] Share with your co-founder or team and determine which step to take next.
- [ ] Once you have one of these steps in action, you can think about incorporating another one or two into your PR strategy.

CHAPTER 11

YOU'VE SECURED COVERAGE, NOW WHAT?

"I never dreamed about success. I worked for it."
- ESTEE LAUDER

That eureka feeling you get after landing a dream feature can quickly wear off when you realize that there is still a lot of work to be done.

While top-tier publications reach millions of people, the traffic can quickly taper off after a few days as it gets lost in the sea of other news.

Don't let this happen to you.

In order to extend the reach of your big media win, it's important to create a plan that you, your team, and community can follow. Don't leave your success in the hands of the overworked journalists. Once you've secured coverage or a media feature, here's how you can keep that momentum going.

1. Promote the Story or Feature

It's surprising how many startups get coverage and then neglect to comment on the article, weigh in, and promote it. Commenting on, or sharing a story that mentions you isn't boastful; it's helpful. It's also polite. The journalist took the time to share your news, so help out by making sure the article gets hits. Repost the story and share it on your channels. Make sure you tag the journalist if you post it on Facebook, and make mention of their name on your other social sites. Publicity is good for your startup, and for the journalist. Relationships are always a two-way street.

According to Kissmetrics, there are specific days of the week and times of day that are best for promoting certain types of content across several different channels. [46] (Kissmetrics, 2011)

You don't need to follow the Kissmetrics' Science of Social Timing to a T, but remember that sharing any news during non-peak hours will decrease your chance of getting your feature in front of more people.

- Promote your piece 2-3 times on the first day on your company and personal Twitter accounts.
- Share it once over the course of the week on your other social media accounts.
- Mention it in your newsletter or throughout your drip email marketing campaigns.
- Write a blog post about it.
- Create lists of forums and communities and start regularly contributing your big wins. Yes, even Reddit is okay with this, provided it's done tactfully and isn't overtly promotional.

2. Publish a Press Page

Oftentimes journalists will refer to your press page to see what's been covered in the past. Venture capitalists also look to media wins to gauge the increase in brand awareness and overall marketing growth of the company. Customers turn to press pages to help make final purchasing decisions. When you're just starting out on this PR journey, you won't have too many wins yet. This means that any mention, link to, interview, or quote from you or your cofounder is still considered press. So start listing all the mentions that you and your company receive. Celebrate them!

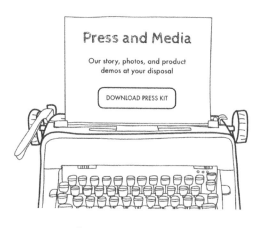

Show Off Your Wins!

3. Write Content That Links to the Recent Media

Sending quality links back to the publications that mentioned or covered you can help you to earn even more brownie points. Take the time to read through, or listen to the content and pull some inspiration for future blog posts or other content forms. Given this is a hot topic now, it's likely that you can get even more traffic if you follow up with something outstanding within the first few days of getting published.

4. Position Yourself As a Go-To Resource in Your Industry

While it may take a bit more than the occasional media mention to be considered an expert, you can mention your recent media wins in your subsequent pitches as a way to establish credibility and expertise.

5. Actively Seek Contributed Author Opportunities

Use your professional perspective as a way to become a contributor author to some relevant publications. Using your top content or top arguments, put together 3-4 blog topic ideas with corresponding bullet points and shop it around to some dream publications. If the ideas don't get picked up, use them for your own blog or video channel.

6. Provide Fresh Data and Statistics

Many writers and journalists look for new and recent data points to use to back up their arguments. Be the startup that runs those reports either quarterly or annually and become a go-to resource for important information in your industry.

Big companies that have a much larger dataset to run reports from will often create proprietary data that they resell back to their community, researchers, and reporters. While you might not be there yet, you may still have some user data that can help either shape a perspective or provide information to help back an argument. Use it to set yourself apart from the competition.

7. Thank Journalists Who Cover You

Never underestimate the power of a simple 'Thank you.' Follow up with any journalist that covers your story just after it goes live. Send them a quick email expressing your thanks. It won't take long, and it shows them that you sincerely appreciate their work. You could even include an excerpt from the article that you especially enjoyed.

Journalists have thankless work. They're constantly being pitched to, and the comments on their stories are sometimes less than encouraging. By expressing your sincere gratitude, you let them know that their work is appreciated, and you'll be fresh in their minds the next time you've got news to share. Relationships will prove to be invaluable, so commit to keeping them alive.

8. Stay in Touch With Your New Contacts

It's vitally important to maintain a connection with the journalists that covered your startup. Share their content, let them call in a favor, assist them with a new story, or top them off about any news you think would benefit them. The idea is to help them out, stay in touch, and help keep your company top of mind. You never know when they might want to pull you into a bigger story. And besides, you might want to pitch to them again in the future.

Remember that getting press coverage is not a one-time thing. It doesn't stop after you get picked up by a couple of news outlets. Media coverage needs to be continual in order to be effective. Ongoing publicity is the best way to keep your startup in the public eye because it increases awareness and leads to that steady stream of new customers you're looking for.

Here are a few ideas for staying connected with journalists:
- Follow their social media accounts.
- Add them to a private Twitter list, so that you can prioritize

communicating with them.
- Respond to their Tweets.
- Read their articles.
- Post comments on their blog posts.
- Drop them the occasional lead about stories that you think they might be interested in.

Maintaining contact shows them that you care, keeps you on their radar, and helps to build your ongoing relationship. Guess what? You'll also stand out to them because of all the effort you're putting in.

Now that you have some great coverage, it can be difficult to secure more media wins without news, so consider how you can sustain the momentum with podcasts, contributed content opportunities, staying in touch with journalists, and helping journalists when you can.

The To Do List:

Take time to reflect on your media wins.

Feel free to stand up and do a little dance. Seriously. We won't tell anyone! Don't forget to share this coverage with your friends and family; your parents will be especially proud.

Don't forget to extend the momentum by doing as many of the following as you can:

- ☐ Promote the story or feature.
- ☐ Publish a press page on your website.
- ☐ Position yourself as a go-to resource.
- ☐ Actively seek contributed author opportunities.
- ☐ Provide fresh data and statistics.
- ☐ Thank journalists who cover you.
- ☐ Stay in touch with your new contacts.

CHAPTER 12

THE CONTINUING ROLE OF PR

"Either write something worth reading, or do something worth writing about."
- BENJAMIN FRANKLIN

If you were to compare PR from years ago to how it is now, you would be surprised at how much has changed, at least on the surface.

In years past, working with a PR professional was one of the only ways for a company to get the connections that they needed to reach the journalists and editors they were looking for. Then along came blogging and social media, and today we find ourselves deep in the age of content creation.

But while a lot has happened in recent years, and the methods for garnering coverage and publicity have changed too, there's one thing that's stayed the same: the tried and true methods of PR – the building blocks of relationships, story development, pitching, and follow-up.

At its heart, PR is –and always will be, about storytelling, and facilitating a connection and conversations between the company and audience; even if our methods must continually adapt to keep up with a changing world.

PR in the Age of Content Creation

Today, we face a constant stream of stories, news, and content. Not just from PR professionals and journalists, but from anyone who has access to the internet. Starting an online business is also easier than ever, with new companies arriving on the scene every day.

But one of the unexpected consequences of all of this competition is that PR has become more important than ever. How else are you going to rise above all of the noise that's out there?

As PR is so integral to the growth of a business, we've seen another new sector emerge as well; 'brand journalists.' These specialists are adept at researching and providing fast turnarounds and have connections within the industry. They're an essential part of the team because their training involves writing for the audience; a key to great storytelling. This new publicist is one who understands the audience and the product; instead of just one or the other.

The best and brightest PR firms are still shaping the content we see online. They are creating, refining, and perfecting stories; distilling them into narratives that are worth telling. They are carefully and strategically working to ensure that the stories will be seen at the opportune time.

A Continuing Challenge

For startups, the start of a new PR journey can be an exciting time, but it's important to begin with realistic expectations; aware of the tremendous amount of work that lies ahead and the potential pitfalls that you might face.

One risk is creating company-centric stories.

Most founders can only think of one story; the reason they created the product or service in the first place. They're keenly aware of why it provides value to them. Startups must continually fight the temptation to write what they want the audience to hear, instead of what needs to be told.

In order to tell your story effectively, you're going to need to think like a publicist, or brand journalist.

Brand journalists can take a founder-centric story and make them accessible to everyone. Great publicists take the time to research and collect data, insights, and case studies in order to present a company's unique positioning standpoint, or their 'why' in a compelling way; in a manner that will appeal to even the most selective journalist. Instead of simply highlighting the basic features of a product or service, they connect the dots and show why the product provides value to an outlet's specific audience. Instead of telling a founder-centric story, they distill the relevant information and create a narrative that reaches everyone; not just the founder or the media outlets.

Another challenge that you'll face is creating consistent content.

It sounds simple enough, but if you've ever tried to create your own content, you know that turning out quality pieces take a lot of time and commitment. At Onboardly, we once calculated that it took an average of 14 hours for an idea to move from the brainstorming stage on to a published blog post. That doesn't even take into account the estimated 80% of the content-creation time that should be given to promotion. The fact is that for many companies, it's simply not enough to have one lone content marketer handling everything from brainstorming and copy to management, budget, and design. But since content marketing costs less than traditional advertising and generates three times as many leads, [47] (McCoy, 2016), many companies find that it's worth enlisting some outside help to ensure that their content is top-notch.

At the end of the day, PR professionals are innate storytellers who are masters at tailoring a story to meet the needs of a media-saturated public. If you're struggling with your narrative, or in your efforts to get your company off the ground, it's worth enlisting the help of a seasoned PR team. Many startups find that they're a key piece of the puzzle and vital for helping their story to stand out and get the attention that it so desperately needs.

Whether you choose to do outreach and promotion yourself or hire a PR team to help you, it's important to ensure that you do your part in getting your company ready for the media. By following the principles that we've outlined in this book, you'll have all of the tools that you need to take on your own PR strategy, or to greatly assist your PR team's efforts, if you decide to outsource it.

CONCLUSION

As quickly as the PR industry changes, there are some things that remain constant.

We thought we'd close this journey into startup PR with a look at some important lessons; things that will help to guide your PR efforts and strategies no matter what changes, innovations, or game-changers arrive on the scene.

Share Stories, Not Features

Great stories last forever. They are your vessel for PR coverage and their significance will only grow as more startups emerge and as media publications continue to operate at overcapacity. There could always be a Google, Facebook, or Uber announcement that may overshadow your company news, so don't rely solely on launches and new features to create a story or get your company noticed. Instead, look to share great stories that cut through the noise; ones that are irresistible to a journalist or writer. These will give your message staying power.

Your 'Why' Is Your North Star

Even though it can be difficult to stay true to it, it's important not to lose sight of your reason. Your 'why' should not only shine through in the stories that you tell, it should also be evident in the conversations you have with your customers and the media. Remind yourself of it daily. It's your key to authenticity in an often-artificial world.

Learn From Your Mistakes

A launch might fail, a journalist may snub you, or a major product launch could overshadow your press announcement. When this happens, it's easy to get frustrated, angry, and lose heart, but it's important to realize that things won't always go as planned. What separates successful startups from everyone else is their ability to recover from setbacks and failures. Try to learn, when there's a lesson to be learned. For everything else, don't take it personally. Instead, dust yourself off, and try again. The PR business requires a thick skin; but the wins, when they're big, will make it all worth it.

Relationships Are Worth Their Weight in Gold

Public relations is exactly that – relations. It's all about building and maintaining relationships; with journalists, your audience, customers, allies, key players, influencers, and more. That will never change. Your secret to long-lasting coverage lies in your ability to nurture connections, constantly build bridges, and always be creating and cultivating relationships. This is your key to PR success.

We truly hope you've enjoyed reading Get Covered and learning our tried, tested, and proven-true PR methodology. Over the years, it's contributed to some fantastic victories, some pretty epic 'we got a win' dances in the office, and most importantly – it's led to really happy startups.

Don't tuck this book into a bookshelf and never reopen it. Always keep it nearby. After all, it's your field guide to navigating the world of PR. Now it's time to go forward, using it, along with the notes that you've taken to help you in your PR journey.

It's your turn in the spotlight now. It's time for you to get covered!

ACKNOWLEDGEMENTS

A books acknowledgements is more than an open opportunity to thank those that have influenced our writing for this book; it's also a chance to acknowledge the dedication and work of those who were there for us from the very beginning.

For myself, Renée, this was my parents and my sister Michelle Warren who encouraged and tutored me as I barely hung on to passing grades in middle school. It's acknowledging the teachers, employers, colleagues, team members and past clients who believed in me while the going was both good and bad.

To my husband Dan Martell for pushing me WAY beyond my comfort zone and allowing me to fail as an entrepreneur often does. You always told me there was a silver lining and, thanks to you, I was able to reach it time and time again throughout my entrepreneurial journey.

To C-star, Crystal, I am so grateful for your patience and support in growing the agency, but in also just believing in me as a person and friend. You are absolutely the best person to co-author this book with, not only because you are incredible, but because your kindness and PR wisdom is really tough to beat. I am so very lucky to have you in my life.

For me, Crystal, it's to 'my' Dan for the countless toffee nut lattes, pizza and love - your unconditional support of my wildest dreams will never cease to amaze me. I'm so glad I met you at Co-Op that one fateful day.

To my mom and dad, from your endless supply of typewriter ink ribbons, which later turned into your patience when I'd sneak out of my bedroom to go write stories on the computer into the late hours of the night - you have both supported my love of storytelling since day one. There isn't a library big enough to house my love and appreciation for you both.

To my tribe and the online storytellers and content creators that inspire me every day - never stop creating.

And to my co-author Renée - I'm so happy I Facebook stalked you years ago. The last five years have been one of my favorite adventures and I can't wait for what we'll get up to next in the #friendzone.

From Renée and Crystal, lastly, but absolutely not the least, to Amanda Fancourt for helping us pull this book all together. To Kandis Gaignard for sifting through the mounds of content and data to stitch together the initial draft and making logic out of a lot of crap. To Rich Gould who helped us through our original design inspiration. And to all of our Onboardly clients over the years who chose us as their agency of choice in helping to launch and grow their businesses. It took an incredible team to make this book come to fruition. We could not have done this without you all. Thank you for your support and inspiration.

ABOUT THE AUTHORS

RENEE WARREN

Renée Warren, a determined realist, is the former founder of popular startup PR firm Onboardly. She's written hundreds of articles and eBooks on startup marketing and has helped some notable clients get on TV shows, magazines, and popular blogs. She is currently on a mission to help over 1 million entrepreneur families gain more freedom in their lives through her program The Family Academy. A certified reiki practitioner, CrossFit athlete and mom to Irish twins, Renée resides on the East coast of Canada with her husband and kids.

CRYSTAL RICHARD

Crystal Richard is the President and Owner of Crystal Richard & Co., a global consulting biz helping startups, entrepreneurs, brands, and small businesses create and tell stories that will attract a tribe of raving fans. A passionate storyteller, Crystal helps entrepreneurs from Cape Town to France to San Francisco get media coverage and bylines in leading online publications such as Entrepreneur, Forbes, the New York Times, Inc. and more. Prior to launching her own company, Crystal was the Director of PR at Onboardly Media. Over her career as a publicist, she has brokered an HGTV pilot, landed a client on the Steve Harvey Show and has taken the stage more than once to speak about storytelling in a digital world. When she isn't brokering media opportunities, Crystal is the blogger behind lifestyle + travel blog East Coast Mermaid where she has partnered with notable tourism and lifestyle brands as a content creator. She will be the first to admit that her cat with thumbs was Instagram famous first.

APPENDIX

Chapter 1: Understanding Public Relations

[1] Chen, A. (n.d.). How To (Actually) Calculate CAC. [Blog] Andrew-Chen. Available at: http://andrewchen.co/how-to-actually-calculate-cac/ [Accessed 1 Nov. 2017]

[2] Ellis, S. (2012). Lean Startup Marketing: Agile Product Development, Business Model Design, Web Analytics, and Other Keys to Rapid Growth. Hyperink

[3] Widrich, L. (2012). The Science of Storytelling: What Listening to a Story Does to Our Brains. [Blog] BufferApp. Available at: https://blog.bufferapp.com/science-of-storytelling-why-telling-a-story-is-the-most-powerful-way-to-activate-our-brains [Accessed 1 Nov. 2017]

[4] Crimmons, L. (2016). 5 Ingredients for a Successful Digital PR Campaign. [PowerPoint slides] Retrieved from: https://www.slideshare.net/LauraCrimmons/sascon-beta-5-ingredients-for-a-successful-digital-pr-campaign [Accessed 1 Nov. 2017]

[5] Marche, S. (2012). Is Facebook Making Us Lonely? The Atlantic. [online] Available at: https://www.theatlantic.com/magazine/archive/2012/05/is-facebook-making-us-lonely/308930/ [Accessed 12 Nov. 2017]

Chapter 2: Executing a Winning PR Strategy: Two Case Studies

[6] Blank, S. G. (2006). The Four Steps to the Epiphany Successful Strategies for Products that Win. Stanford. [online] Available at: http://web.stanford.edu/group/e145/cgi-bin/winter/drupal/upload/handouts/Four_Steps.pdf [Accessed 1 Nov. 2017]

Chapter 3: Are You Ready for PR?

[7] Alexander, L., (2016). Why it's time to retire 'disruption', Silicon Valley's emptiest buzzword. The Guardian. [online] Available at: https://www.theguardian.com/technology/2016/jan/11/disruption-silicon-valleys-buzzword [Accessed 1 Nov. 2017]

[8] Walsham, T., (2015). How to save your early-stage startup from certain doom. [PowerPoint slides] Retrieved from: https://www.slideshare.net/startupfest/startupfest-2015-tom-walsham-twg-how-to-stage [Accessed 12 Nov. 2017]

Chapter 4: Crafting the Ultimate Story

[9] Cron, L. (2013). Wired for Story: The Writer's Guide to Using Brain Science to Hook Readers from the Very First Sentence. New York: Ten Speed Press

[10] Murray, P.N. PhD (2013). How Emotions Influence What We Buy: The emotional core of consumer decision-making. [Blog] Psychology Today. Available at: https://www.psychologytoday.com/blog/inside-the-consumer-mind/201302/how-emotions-influence-what-we-buy [Accessed 1 Nov. 2017]

[11] Lee, K. (2015). The Complete, Actionable Guide to Marketing Personas. [Blog] BufferApp. Available at: https://blog.bufferapp.com/mar-

keting-personas-beginners-guide [Accessed 29 Oct. 2017]

[12] Points, F., (2011). Five Strategies for Speaking to B2B Buyers' Pain Points. [Blog] MarketingProfs. Available at: http://www.marketingprofs.com/articles/2011/5920/five-strategies-for-speaking-to-b2b-buyers-pain-points [Accessed 1 Nov. 2017]

[13] Putnam, J. (2012). What a Unique Selling Proposition Really Means & Why Your Business MUST Have One. [Blog] Kissmetrics. Available at: https://blog.kissmetrics.com/unique-selling-proposition/ [Accessed 1 Nov. 2017]

[14] Rush, B.C. (2014). Science of storytelling: why and how to use it in your marketing. The Guardian. [online] Available at: http://www.theguardian.com/media-network/media-network-blog/2014/aug/28/science-storytelling-digital-marketing [Accessed 1 Nov. 2017]

[15] Godin, S. (2006). Ode: How to tell a great story. [Blog] SethGodin. Available at: http://sethgodin.typepad.com/seths_blog/2006/04/ode_how_to_tell.html [Accessed 1 Nov. 2017]

[16] Gladwell, M. (2007). Blink: The Power of Thinking Without Thinking. Little, Brown and Company

[17] 15Five, (n.d.). 15Five Story. [online] Available at: https://www.15five.com/about/15five-story/ [Accessed 1 Nov. 2017]

[18] Read, A. (2016). The Secrets To Combatting Content Overload: How To Craft Content People Love. [Blog] BufferApp. Available at: https://blog.bufferapp.com/content-overload [Accessed 1 Nov. 2017]

[19] Puranjay, S. (2015). 2 Million Blog Posts Are Written Every Day, Here's How You Can Stand Out. [Blog] MarketingProf. Available at: http://www.marketingprofs.com/articles/2015/27698/2-million-blog-posts-are-written-every-day-heres-how-you-can-stand-out [Accessed 1 Nov. 2017]

[20] Business Insider, (2011). How Many Contacts Does It Take Before

Someone Buys Your Product? [online] Available at: http://www.businessinsider.com/how-many-contacts-does-it-take-before-someone-buys-your-product-2011-7 [Accessed 29 Oct, 2017]

Chapter 6: Establishing Goals and Tracking Your PR Efforts

[21, 27, 32] AirPR, (n.d.). PR Measurement. [online] Available at: https://www.airpr.com/pr-measurement [Accessed 29 Oct. 2017]

[22] Nielsen, (2015). Global Trust in Advertising. [online] Available at: http://www.nielsen.com/us/en/insights/reports/2015/global-trust-in-advertising-2015.html [Accessed 29 Oct. 2017]

[23, 28, 30] TrendKite, (n.d.). How to Build a PR Report Your Company Will Actually Like. [online] Available at: http://www.trendkite.com/hubfs/eBooks/How_to_build_a_PR_report_your_company_will_like/trendkite-ebook-how-to-build-a-pr-report-your-company-will-like.pdf [Accessed 29 Oct. 2017]

[24, 25, 26] Ketchum Global Research & Analytics, (n.d). The Principles of PR Measurement. [online] Available at: https://www.ketchum.com/sites/default/files/insights/ketchum_white_paper_principles-pr-measurement.pdf [Accessed 29 Oct, 2017]

[29, 31, 34] PR Daily, (2014). Four PR metrics you can start using today. [online] Available at: http://www.prdaily.com/Main/Articles/Four_PR_metrics_you_can_start_using_today_16237.aspx [Accessed 5 Nov. 2017]

[33] Cision, (2014). Measuring for Impact: Metrics that Matter. [online] Available at: http://www.cision.com/us/2014/09/measuring-for-impact-metrics-that-matter/ [Accessed 5 Nov. 2017]

Chapter 7: Start Building Rapport Early

[35] Fast Company, (2014). Defining The Future Of Public Relations. [online] Available at: https://www.fastcompany.com/3036158/defining-the-future-of-public-relations [Accessed 5 Nov. 2017]

Chapter 8: Perfecting Your Pitch

[36] Libert, K. (2014). Get Your Pitch Noticed by a Major Publisher. Harvard Business Review. [online] Available at: https://hbr.org/2014/10/get-your-pitch-noticed-by-a-major-publisher [Accessed 5 Nov. 2017]

Chapter 9: Be Prepared: Are You Ready for When the Media Comes Knocking?

[37] Warren, R. (2016). How to be Ready for the Spotlight: The Founder's Guide to Looking Ridiculously Good Online. [Blog] Onboardly. http://onboardly.com/thought-leaders/ready-spotlight-founders-guide-looking-ridiculously-good-online/ [Accessed 5 Nov. 2017]

[38] 15Five, (n.d.). 15Five Story. [online] Available at: https://www.15five.com/about/15five-story/ [Accessed 1 Nov. 2017]

[39] Onboardly, (n.d.). Rent frock Repeat Media Kit. [online] http://marketing.onboardly.com/hubfs/rfr.pdf [Accessed 29 Oct. 2017]

[40] Uber, (n.d.). Media. [online] https://www.uber.com/media/ [Accessed 29 Oct. 2017]

[41] Trulia, (n.d.). Info. [online] http://info.trulia.com [Accessed 29 Oct. 2017]

Chapter 10: Gaining Traction When the Media Won't Cover You

[42] First Round, (n.d.). Why Most Startups Don't 'Get' Press. [online] Available at: http://firstround.com/review/why-most-startups-dont-get-press/ [Accessed 5 Nov. 2017]

[43] Scott, D. M. (n.d.). Newsjacking. [online] Available at: http://www.davidmeermanscott.com/books/newsjacking/ [Accessed 5 Nov. 2017]

[44] ABC News, (2011) NT insures Obama against croc attack. [online] Available at: http://www.abc.net.au/news/2011-11-15/obama-given-croc-insurance/3673476 [Accessed 5 Nov. 2017]

[45] Michael Hyatt, (n.d.) Speaking. [online] Available at: https://michaelhyatt.com/speaking [Accessed 29 Oct. 2017]

Chapter 11: You've Secured Coverage, Now What?

[46] Kissmetrics, (2011). The Science of Social Timing Part 3: Timing and Blogging. [online] Available at: https://blog.kissmetrics.com/science-of-social-timing-3/ [Accessed 29 Oct. 2017]

Chapter 12: The Continuing Role of PR

[47] McCoy, J. (2016). Why is Content Marketing Today's Marketing? 10 Stats That Prove It. [Blog] Content Marketing Institute. Available at: http://contentmarketinginstitute.com/2016/08/content-marketing-stats/ [Accessed 29 Oct. 2017]

Made in the USA
Monee, IL
14 March 2022